✫✫✫✫✫✫✫✫✫✫✫✫✫✫✫✫

**BASEBALL
SUPERSTARS**

Ichiro Suzuki

✫✫✫✫✫✫✫✫✫✫✫✫✫✫✫✫

BASEBALL SUPERSTARS

Ichiro Suzuki

Judith Levin

CHELSEA HOUSE
PUBLISHERS
An imprint of Infobase Publishing

For Brian

ICHIRO SUZUKI

Chelsea House
An imprint of Infobase Publishing
132 West 31st Street
New York NY 10001

Library of Congress Cataloging-in-Publication Data
Levin, Judith (Judith N.), 1956-
  Ichiro Suzuki / Judith Levin.
    p. cm. — (Baseball superstars)
  Includes bibliographical references and index.
  ISBN-13: 978-0-7910-9440-2 (hardcover)
  ISBN-10: 0-7910-9440-5 (hardcover)
  1. Suzuki, Ichiro, 1973—Juvenile literature. 2. Baseball players—Japan—Biography—Juvenile literature. 3. Baseball players—United States—Biography—Juvenile literature. I. Title. II. Series.
  GV865.S895L48 2007
  796.357092—dc22
  [B]   2007005920

Chelsea House books are available at special discounts when purchased in bulk quantities for businesses, associations, institutions, or sales promotions. Please call our Special Sales Department in New York at (212) 967-8800 or (800) 322-8755.

You can find Chelsea House on the World Wide Web at http://www.chelseahouse.com

Series design by Erik Lindstrom
Cover design by Ben Peterson

Printed in the United States of America

Bang EJB 10 9 8 7 6 5 4 3 2 1

This book is printed on acid-free paper.

All links and Web addresses were checked and verified to be correct at the time of publication. Because of the dynamic nature of the Web, some addresses and links may have changed since publication and may no longer be valid.

CONTENTS

Ichiro-mania

It was just a typical game for Ichiro Suzuki. It was a little more than halfway through the 2006 season, at the end of a three-game series between the Seattle Mariners and the New York Yankees. It was a hot July day game, with the cheap seats at Yankee Stadium full of the bright T-shirts worn by groups of kids from summer camps.

As the leadoff hitter for Seattle, Ichiro came to the plate, performing his trademark warm-ups and stretches. The first pitch from the Yankees' Randy Johnson brushed him back. Johnson had worn No. 51 for Seattle before Ichiro inherited it in 2001. The second pitch, Ichiro hit for a clean single. Within a few minutes, teammate Adrián Beltré hit a double and Ichiro was home, practically before the spectators in the bleachers were done finding their seats.

Ichiro Suzuki of the Seattle Mariners slid safely into second after stealing the base in the eighth inning of a game on July 19, 2006, against the New York Yankees. The hurried throw from Yankee catcher Kelly Stinnett bounced in front of second baseman Miguel Cairo (left) and rolled into center field. Suzuki took third base on the error.

1-0, Mariners.

At his second at-bat, in the third inning, Ichiro hit a single, then promptly stole second. That time he was left stranded, when Beltré struck out to end the inning. By the eighth inning, the score was 2-2, and Ichiro was leading off again. What followed was "pretty vintage" Ichiro, said Seattle manager Mike Hargrove. Suzuki hit the top of a hard-breaking slider and drove it all of about 15 feet (4.6 meters). By the time Yankee catcher Kelly Stinnett (regular catcher Jorge Posada was on the disabled list with a hurt finger) and Johnson converged on the ball, Ichiro was safe on first. Then, before Stinnett could settle himself down, Ichiro stole second and—on Stinnett's rushed, bouncing overthrow to second—stole third. He then scored on a sacrifice fly. The game would end 3-2 in favor of the Mariners, with Ichiro having scored two runs. He had three hits and three stolen bases. His batting average as of the end of the game was .343. And the Mariners were still in last place in the American League West.

"Dazed, Confused, and Then Defeated" read the headline in the *New York Times* the next day. "The Yankees did not know whether to be exasperated or awed," Lee Jenkins wrote. In Ichiro's sixth season in the majors, no one had figured out how to slow him down. He had never had a season in which he batted below .300. Although opponents had ceased to be surprised by Ichiro's infield hits, they still could not field them—he got to base too fast. He seemed to be running almost before he was done hitting.

It was one more afternoon of vindication for the player who most of American baseball said would never make it in the major leagues.

THE FIRST JAPANESE POSITION PLAYER

When the Seattle Mariners signed Ichiro Suzuki in the fall of 2000, he was the first Japanese position player to sign a major-league contract. Other Japanese players had come to the United States, starting with Hideo Nomo in 1995, but they had all been pitchers. "The Japanese can't hit major-league pitchers" is what practically everyone said. Ichiro—already playing pro ball in Japan with his first name on the back of his jersey, so famous that he had his own clothing line and had come to the United States to marry his Japanese girlfriend in peace—was Japan's test case. At five feet nine inches tall and 156 pounds (175 centimeters and 71 kilograms), the record-breaking right fielder was still assumed to be, like his countrymen, too small to play with the big boys of the major leagues. No matter how good he had been in Japan, he would not be good enough here. Rob Dibble, an ESPN Radio sports announcer, said in April 2001 that he would strip naked and run through Times Square if Ichiro won a batting title. That June, Lou Piniella, then the Mariners' manager, told him, "Better start working on your tan."

Long before that "vintage" game of his sixth season, Ichiro had put to rest the question of whether Japanese position players could make it in the majors. "Too small" and "not strong enough" had been replaced by "graceful and gritty" and also by "frustrating" (for opposing teams). Other Japanese position players had come to the majors, and the games they played were all broadcast on television and radio in Japan. Ichiro had started that. When he began to play for the Mariners, their games started to attract more Japanese fans than Japan's own baseball league.

In his first season, Ichiro rapidly took on something of a legendary quality, for his infield singles, for his running swing, his rocket throws, his speedy steals, and for his almost eerie ability to hit the ball where he wanted. (By the time of that 2006 game, an announcer would say of a well-placed ball by a Yankee hitter, "He's going to out-Ichiro Ichiro if he keeps that up.") Fans and historians of baseball began to speak of Ichiro as someone likely to be the first player to bat over .400 since Ted Williams hit .406 in 1941.

In addition, Ichiro got everyone's attention for his idiosyncratic batting stance and a swing so odd that it had kept him benched during the beginning of his pro career in Japan. He came to the ballpark hours before his teammates to warm up, and he performed odd-looking limbering-up exercises and stretches before each game and before each at-bat. Little League ballplayers across the United States were soon imitating his expressionless pretzeling of his body.

Some of the Ichiro legend was fueled by his inaccessibility to the press. It is partly because he came to the United States speaking only Japanese—he has now added a fair amount of English and Spanish, but he still uses a translator during interviews. It is partly because, much of the time, he would rather not speak to the press at all. Ever since his first spring training, his answers to questions have mystified people. When asked what he called the six-inch stick with which he massaged the soles of his feet after each game, he replied, "Wood." When asked his dog's name, he said he did not have the dog's permission to answer that. When asked to discuss a spectacular catch

☆ ☆ ☆ ☆ ☆ ☆

ICHIRO BOBBLEHEADS

One small measure of Ichiro's popularity is the number of years that Ichiro bobblehead dolls have been distributed and the popularity of those dolls. Because only 25,000 are given out, Ichiro Bobblehead Day has caused fans to line up around the block hours before game time—in 2001, they camped overnight to receive one.

The 2001 bobblehead showed a rather chubby Ichiro. The 2002 doll portrayed a slimmer Ichiro as a batter, in honor of his 2001 MVP award. It showed him with his bat held toward the pitcher, parallel to his body, his left hand adjusting the shoulder of his right sleeve.

The 2003 doll honored Ichiro's Gold Glove. It portrayed him catching a ball just above the outfield wall, looking cool in his sunglasses. In 2005, the bobblehead honored the 262 hits Ichiro had gotten the year before, breaking George Sisler's season record.

The 2006 doll showed Ichiro running. Because that doll was designed before the season started, it did not reflect his choice to wear shorter pants and high socks all season.

that involved plucking a home-run ball from above the fence (then hitting the ground, doing a backward somersault, and adjusting his sunglasses), he said, "It was a fly ball. I caught it."

Was he angry? Zen? Joking? Annoying the reporters on purpose? No one knew what to make of him. He was a mystery. He was a superstar known only by his first name, like Tiger or Madonna or Elvis. He wore baggy pants and gel-spiked hair and $495 sunglasses, and he listened to rap and hip-hop. He was so famous that mail addressed to "Ichiro, Japan" would be delivered to him. Rumors persisted that one Japanese newspaper had offered $1 million for a nude picture of him. He did not act like a superstar, however. During his first season, he initially refused to pose for the cover of *Sports Illustrated*, saying, "I haven't done anything yet."

Baseball fans thought he had done plenty. He made headlines for a 200-foot (67-meter) throw from right field to third base so perfect that sportswriters vied with one another to describe it. It was a bullet, a rocket, a throw so amazing that "it should be in the Louvre next to the *Mona Lisa*." Finally it was just "The Throw." Safeco Field, the home of the Mariners, was soon selling an Ichi-roll (of spicy tuna) at its sushi bars and hiring Japanese-speaking vendors to serve the thousands of visitors who came from Japan to watch their Ichiro in the "Bigs." The Mariners were also selling more merchandise featuring his name or picture than they ever had of any other player. "Ichiro-mania," as the media called it, was in full swing. The first Japanese position player in the major leagues won Rookie of the Month honors four times during his first season, he was named Rookie of the Year, and he led in votes for the All-Star team of the American League. He won a Gold Glove and the American League's Most Valuable Player (MVP) award. Right field was christened "Area 51."

And one cold December night in 2001, Rob Dibble ran through Times Square wearing nothing but his Speedo.

Ichiro's Childhood

In 2000, Ichiro's father opened the "Ichiro Exhibition Room" in Toyoyama, Japan, a few blocks from the small house where Ichiro grew up. People have plenty of different responses to the huge collection of objects, but a common one is, "Didn't they ever throw anything out?" Gleaming, pristine cabinets show off Ichiro's childhood toys, including Nintendo games, Bruce Lee action figures, Transformer toys, and his *Go* game board. Pictures of Ichiro from infancy to the present day are displayed, as is a collection of more than 100 scrapbooks of clippings about him, starting with ones from his earliest Little League appearances. There is a mannequin of Ichiro at age 12 sitting at the desk he used when he was a kid, doing math on his abacus. Also, his school essays and report cards, all his uniforms and equipment, his shoes (and shoe polish), and the bats he splintered learning to play baseball. His bicycle is there; so is his dental retainer. Aside from the 2,000 to 3,000 items on display, nearly 3,000 more are in storage.

The museum's manager says, "When Ichiro was a child, his father told Ichiro's mother, 'He is going to be a great athlete. We must keep everything.'" So they did—from October 22, 1973, when he was born, until now.

The story of Ichiro's childhood has become a legend, a bigger-than-life tale told over and over again in numerous Japanese and English books and articles. It is the story of a little boy whose life was dedicated to the game of baseball—dedicated by himself or by an ambitious father.

THE RED GLOVE

The story starts with the red baseball glove. Not a toy, Ichiro says, but a real leather baseball glove and a ball that his father gave to him when he was three years old. It was the most expensive glove available in their town, costing about half of what Nobuyuki Suzuki earned in a month as manager of a small factory that made electrical parts. The glove was the first of many investments of time and money that Mr. Suzuki would make in his small son. Why Ichiro? Why not his older brother? No one ever says. Ichiro's father, though, must have seen something in his second son that made him hope that his own dream of becoming a professional ballplayer could come true for the tot. (He might have seen superb eye-hand coordination. Ichiro had it, and that has to be inborn as well as developed.)

Mr. Suzuki began to play catch every day with Ichiro. The boy carried his red glove with him everywhere. It was at this time that his father began the first of many rituals associated with the game and the equipment used to play it. At the end of each game of catch, the boy had to clean and oil his glove. It was not a toy, it was equipment, and it was to be treated with "respect and gratitude." By the time Ichiro started nursery school, he was a fan of the local pro team, the Chunichi Dragons. (Japanese professional teams are named after the companies that own them, not after the place in which they play.) In first grade, he began to play on the local Little League team, a full two years younger than was allowed. He would soon be so good that he could get hits off the fifth and sixth graders. The baseball team practiced only once a week, so Ichiro asked his father to coach him. His father made him promise that he would keep at it and practice every day. Ichiro agreed, though perhaps he did not fully understand what he was agreeing to.

PRACTICE MAKES PERFECT

By the time Ichiro was nine, Mr. Suzuki was leaving work every day at 3:30 P.M., when school got out, and he and Ichiro would jog to the neighborhood Little League field. Every day, year-round, they would play catch. Then Ichiro would throw pitches (perhaps 50) and long balls. As a child, he was a pitcher. He would hit off the tee and hit balls his father pitched to him (about 200). Infield and outfield defensive practice followed, as his father hit 100 or more fungoes. Then Ichiro would collect the red hard-rubber balls that Japanese children play baseball with and the other equipment and would carry them home. On their way home, Ichiro was usually rewarded with ice cream.

After dinner and homework, Ichiro and his father would go to a batting center and Ichiro would take 250 to 300 pitches from the machine. Early on—so early that he says he cannot remember it—the right-hander was taught by his father to bat left for the advantage it would give him getting to first base. The speed of the pitches he could hit grew as he did. At eight, he practiced on 65-mile-per-hour (105-kilometer-per-hour) pitches—curveballs and screwballs, as well as fastballs. By the end of elementary school, he practiced on balls thrown at the machine's fastest speed, 75 miles per hour (121 kilometers per hour). Within a couple of years,

Nobuyuki Suzuki, the father of Ichiro Suzuki, spoke to reporters in Toyoyama, Japan, in October 2004, after Ichiro broke the major-league record for most hits in a season. Mr. Suzuki gave Ichiro his first glove when the boy was three years old. For several years, he intensely drilled Ichiro daily on his batting and fielding.

even those posed no challenge to him. First, the staff at the batting center added a spring that created 80-mile-per-hour (129-kilometer-per-hour) pitches. (The spring is in the Ichiro museum.) Finally, when Ichiro was 15, the machine itself was moved closer to him, so that the pitches were coming at the equivalent of 93 miles per hour (150 kilometers per hour). At that time, 93 miles per hour was as fast as the fastest pro pitcher in Japan could throw. Ichiro and his father were often still there when the batting center closed at 11 P.M. Then, home at last, Mr. Suzuki massaged the bottoms of Ichiro's feet, for circulation and health.

REBELLION

It was a tough schedule for an elementary school student. Ichiro had agreed to it, but sometimes he would rebel. But when he would say he did not want to practice, his father would simply say, "You'd better come," and the boy would follow. Once Ichiro started a practice session, he would generally enjoy it. Still, it was hard. Sometimes at the end, he would lie down on the field and refuse to move, and when his father left him, he would go home the long way, hoping to make his father worry. He once staged a sit-down strike when his father refused to let him leave early to play with his friends. Mr. Suzuki responded by throwing balls at his son—hard. He tells this story himself in his book *My Son, Ichiro*. Ichiro proved his talent that day by dodging the balls thrown at him at close range and catching the ones he could not otherwise escape. Mr. Suzuki was proud, but Ichiro did not get to play with his friends that day.

It was all good fun, his father would say later. Ichiro disagrees. Asked about his early training, he says it bordered on hazing—or on child abuse. Reminded by one Japanese-speaking American interviewer of his father's description of their practices as fun, Ichiro switched abruptly from Japanese to English to say, "He lies." Japanese is not an easy language in which to call your father a liar.

Still, Ichiro shows no signs of regretting his early training. Of course he did not always like it, he says, especially when it was so cold that his fingers went numb and he could not do up his buttons. But his father—locally nicknamed "the 3:30 man" for his habitual early departure from work—gave up all his free time, too, and even his beloved golf games to work with his son. Mr. Suzuki devised the "life-or-death drill" for his son, pitching hard, professional-quality balls from only a few yards away to Ichiro, who had to hit them to the right or left of his father so as not to injure him. The chance of being concussed by a badly hit ball was less important to Mr. Suzuki than the concentration and bat control that the drill gave his son.

Ichiro attributes much of his success to his father's work with him. He says that his "feel" for the game comes from those early drills. He especially appreciates that his father let him develop his own style of hitting, while a regular coach would have put him into a mold, telling him how to stand and how to swing. His father instead encouraged him to imitate his favorite players, like Kazunori Shinozuka from the Tokyo Yomiuri Giants (as a batter) and Tatsuo Komatsu of the Chunichi Dragons (as a pitcher). He was able to incorporate elements of their style into his own, learning from trial and error what felt right to him. His father also taught him techniques that a regular coach would not have. His early golf-like "pendulum" swing was partly the result of his father's admiration for the female pro golfer Ayako Okamoto. Mr. Suzuki thought that the shift from one foot to the other would put Ichiro's full weight behind his swing, and it did.

Of course, Ichiro's "full weight" still was not much. Although he was strong and well muscled, he remained slight. In part, that was just his body type, but he did not help by being a fussy eater. He did not like to eat vegetables, and his favorite foods were among the most expensive ones in the Japanese diet—Kobe beef (it is more than $100 a pound in the United States) and sashimi. Overriding Mrs. Suzuki, Ichiro's father said the boy could have all of these delicacies if he would also drink a lot of milk.

"CONCENTRATION"

When Ichiro was in sixth grade, he wrote an essay for school about baseball. (The essay is in the Ichiro museum). He wrote that from age 9 he had practiced 360 days a year and that he dreamed of becoming a professional ballplayer, preferably for the Seibu Lions or the Chunichi Dragons. "My goal is a contract signing bonus of 100 million yen," he wrote. "If I become one of the best baseball players in the future, I'm going to give tickets to all my friends and family and everyone who helped me. Then if they come to the stadium they can cheer me." The word *shūchū*, meaning "concentration," was written on his glove.

Ichiro started junior high school in 1985, as a pitcher who threw right-handed and batted left-handed. Although his father's work with him was not over, Ichiro would now be part of a school team and be trained by its coach. His father told the coach not to change Ichiro's batting form. He also said, "No matter how good Ichiro is, don't ever praise him. We have to make him spiritually strong." Mr. Suzuki had not praised Ichiro, either. No "good job, son." He did not tell Ichiro how talented he was, although he would occasionally "make some offhand comment about it," Ichiro said later. "That made me so happy and was a great encouragement." Yet Ichiro knew unquestioningly that his father was there for him. Mr. Suzuki showed up every day to watch Ichiro's after-school team practice. After dinner, they still went to the batting center. Ichiro did his homework after it closed. His father stayed up with him, in case he needed help, and they would finish around 2 in the morning—with a foot massage.

In junior high, Ichiro was successful as a student and as a baseball player. "Even if I wasn't paying attention in class, I'd cram for tests and do great," he would later tell an interviewer. Additionally, his father's supervision of his homework ensured that he had completed it. At the end of his three years of junior high school, Ichiro had earned top grades as well as produced the best pitching, hitting, and fielding records on the school team. He could have gone to a high school that would have prepared him for Japan's best and most prestigious university. Of course, he chose baseball over academics and was admitted to Aiko-Dai Meiden High School in nearby Nagoya, a school with a long history of excellent baseball teams. The school had produced a number of pro baseball players.

HIGH SCHOOL BALL

High school is not a fun time for Japanese students but rather a time when their characters are supposed to be shaped by adults. The top academic high schools in Japan are famous for their toughness and competitiveness as they prepare Japanese students for difficult college-entrance exams. At the prestigious colleges, however, students are expected to socialize and relax. Before college age, say the Japanese, a child's character has been formed and his or her work habits honed.

Baseball, like Japanese martial arts, is considered important as a discipline. Suishu Tobita, a well-known college baseball manager and columnist in Japan, once wrote, "The purpose of training is the forging of the soul. If the players do not try so hard as to vomit blood in practice, they cannot hope to win games. One must suffer to be good." The good high school teams were organized in this same spirit. Most essential—more important than winning, even—were the life lessons. When Ichiro arrived at high school, his manager, Go Nakamura, told him, "For the rest of your life you'll never experience anything as tough as what you're going to go through now." Ichiro thought, "Well, we'll see." It was, he said later, "the hardest thing

I've ever experienced"—even harder than his later training as a pro. Nakamura also said, "How can someone this scrawny play ball?"—at least that is what Ichiro later heard he had said.

Ichiro and the other 50 students in the baseball program lived at the school eleven months a year during their three years of high school. (They lived at home in January.) The facilities were excellent. The dormitory included weight-training rooms, and the ball field was as good as a professional one. The dormitory also included a kitchen and a laundry room in which the students did their own cooking and laundry. The students also cared for the field. (In Japan, pro players have some responsibilities for taking care of the field and their equipment, too.)

Only the 17 best (and older) members of the team did not have to cook and do laundry. Like the others, Ichiro in his first year cooked for the older students, did their laundry for them, and ran their baths after dinner. This was part of the philosophy of forging the spirits of the baseball players, as individual players and as a team. Learning to play ball was not just a matter of hitting or fielding but included learning respect for more senior players, for the field, and for the equipment. It was the same philosophy that had led Mr. Suzuki to teach his three-year-old son to clean and oil his glove after each game of catch and that caused him, now, to bow to his son's baseball field as he left each day.

There exists in Japan something called the *totei seido*, the apprenticeship system, not just in sports or schools but in businesses and in government offices. People become part of a team or a company by working their way up in it. This is not unfamiliar—after all, the practice of working your way up a hierarchy exists in European and American companies, too—but in the Japanese system, the sense of a gradual rise and of enormous respect for the system and for those above you runs far deeper. At Ichiro's school, it was considered appropriate and necessary for older students to discipline younger ones. A lack of respect or a failure to wash the rice properly before cooking it—or for Ichiro, getting caught with an ice cream cone he had bought—would result in punishments, such as making a player crouch on top of a small garbage can with his legs tucked under him and his weight on his calves and feet. It was agony.

Ichiro did not complain, and, he says, he did not think much about it. "I was so totally focused on baseball I didn't have time to worry about anything else," he said later. "You just grin and bear it and accept things as they are." Also, he agreed with his coaches that this training was the best for him as a player. He says that Mr. Nakamura was the greatest teacher he had ever had, teaching him lessons about life as well as about baseball. The harshness of the training was not to injure the spirits of the player—or in American terms, to injure their self-esteem—but, as Ichiro's father had told his son's junior high school coach, to make their spirits strong.

As a first-year student, Ichiro simply did what was necessary to fulfill his responsibilities to the older players while preparing himself as a player. Rather than wait in long lines for the washing machines, he got up at 3 A.M. to do the laundry. This freed him to practice after dinner. He slept in class.

MAKING THE TEAM

Ichiro made the top 17 players in his junior year. Rice-cooking and laundry were now jobs for the younger guys, and he was free to train all the time he did not have to be in class. Practice was from 3:30 to 8 P.M., followed by dinner, with batting practice beginning at 9. Some of the team's drills included strength exercises like hitting Wiffle balls with a heavy shovel and throwing car tires.

Ichiro's father attended home games, away games, and practices. Often he would watch without speaking. At other times, he took Ichiro to see the fields where the away games would be played. He also brought with him hip-hop tapes that Ichiro's older brother had mixed for him.

It is hard to say what Ichiro's teammates thought of him. Even as a child he showed little emotion during games, never cheering or jumping up and down after a good play as his

★ ☆ ★ ☆ ★ ☆

A STORIED COMPETITION

Here in the United States, high school sports of all sorts—football, basketball, soccer, lacrosse—are popular with students, parents, and other fans. Rarely, though, does this popularity achieve the heights of the Kōshien baseball tournaments in Japan. The competition attracts up to a million spectators to Kōshien Stadium in Nishinomiya, near Kobe, Japan. Millions more watch on television, including many who generally pay scant attention to professional baseball in Japan.

The fabled tournament, almost a century old, is actually two tournaments—informally known as Spring Kōshien and Summer Kōshien. Spring Kōshien, which takes place in March, is the smaller of the contests. It is an invitation-only tournament, with a field of 32 high school teams.

In essence, Summer Kōshien has a field of more than 4,000 teams. Beginning in June, regional tournaments are held in each of Japan's prefectures, which are regional government divisions similar to states. Summer Kōshien culminates with a two-week tourney in August featuring 49 teams—they represent all of the prefectures, with two teams from Tokyo, Japan's largest city, and Hokkaidō, the country's largest prefecture.

Among Kōshien's millions of fans are the throngs of high school students who come to support their teams. These groups—with brass bands, drummers, and cheerleaders—sit in designated cheering areas, and the bands play only when their team is batting. These student fans are as well organized as the ball teams.

teammates did. As a high school player, his game face was intact—so intact that his classmates called him "spaceman" or "no weather." Although Ichiro has protested at various times that, of course, he has emotions and gets nervous like everyone else, he also has the ability to calm and discipline himself under pressure. The evidence is in the way he plays. His average during his three years of high school was .502. Then, as now, he was also known for how seldom he struck out: only 10 times in 536 high school at-bats, and he never went down swinging. Additionally, his mental calm was actually measured by university researchers doing a study in which they used brain-wave activity to judge the ability of athletes to relax under pressure. The average for other athletes was 60 percent. Ichiro, tested 10 times during a 10-month period in high school, scored 91 percent.

In high school, Ichiro had some success as a pitcher, but he was not the team's star in that area. Then, in his second year, he was hit by a car while riding his bike. His right calf was injured, and he spent one and a half months on crutches. When he was able to play ball again, he played first base for a while. After that, he could not get back his form as a pitcher: He would hit himself in the head with the ball before he could release it. It was not until several years into his pro career that he felt secure in his throwing.

THE KŌSHIEN TOURNAMENT

The goal of Japanese high school baseball teams and of players who hope to become pros is to compete in the annual tournament in Kōshien Stadium, near Kobe. Of the thousands of high school teams, all but 49 are eliminated in regional tournaments. Those 49 participate in one of Japan's most popular sporting events, famous since it began in 1916. Not only does the stadium hold more than 50,000 people, but all two weeks of the competition are televised nationally. Scouts for the pro teams watch it closely.

Baseball players from 32 high schools marched during the opening ceremony of the Spring Kōshien tournament in March 2004 in Nishinomiya, Japan. The Kōshien tournaments—a bigger one is played in the summer—attract millions of spectators who watch in person or on television.

Ichiro participated in the Kōshien tournament in the summer of his second year of high school and in the spring of his third (and last) year. (The spring tournament is smaller but still important and popular.) He did not like the experience very much. He found himself awed and a bit overwhelmed by the stadium, which has stands so high that it is nicknamed "the Alps." Knowing that the game was being televised made him nervous, too, and he felt he was not "able to play up to [his] potential." (He batted .625 in the spring tourney.) The team was eliminated in the first round, and Ichiro was—true to his nicknames—the only player on his team who did not cry.

The games that mattered even more to Ichiro were the ones that were part of his prefectural (regional) championship in his last summer of high school. These games were the last chance that the pro scouts would have to look at him before the fall drafts began. Ichiro set himself a characteristically simple goal: to bat 1.000 during the championship. He managed a measly .750 instead.

The pro scouts indeed took notice of Ichiro, not only of his performance in the prefectural championship but also of his high school record. Yet even with his great statistics, he was drafted only in the fourth and last round. At five feet nine inches tall and 120 pounds, he was a skinny baseball player and he looked about 11 years old. Nevertheless, in November 1991, the Orix BlueWave selected Ichiro Suzuki as an outfielder.

The History
of Baseball
in Japan

It is not possible to understand Ichiro Suzuki simply by say-ing, "Well, he's Japanese." Of course, all Japanese baseball players are not alike. After all, it was not teens from Iowa who called Ichiro "spaceman" and "no weather" because of his apparent emotional detachment. It was other Japanese teens, raised at the same time and place as he was. Other Japanese Little Leaguers jumped up and down with excitement during games or cried with disappointment. He did not.

At the same time, it is not possible to understand Ichiro without understanding that he is part of Japanese culture and part of a long tradition of Japanese baseball. Each year at the Little League World Series, the Japanese players bow to the field and to their parents. They conduct themselves efficiently and professionally, and the commentators always speak of their grasp of "fundamentals" and their self-discipline. They work together closely "almost like the parts of a machine" and seem "businesslike." And they make few mental or physical errors. These kids have been drilled *hard*. Ichiro grew up in that tradition of baseball.

So, yes, he is Japanese, but he is also himself. He is the product of a particular set of genes and of a father who had wanted to play ball and could not and so was able to carry out his dream through his son. Ichiro's determination to get better and better all the time—his thoroughness—is both cultural and his own.

"STAR OF THE GIANTS"

People who tell Ichiro's story always refer to a famous Japanese comic strip series, "Star of the Giants." It ran in newspapers in the 1960s and then was on television. The Giants are the Tokyo Yomiuri Giants, the Japanese team that is sort of the Yankees of pro ball in Japan. The Giants have a history of high payrolls and of winning the Japan Series, the Japanese equivalent of the major-league World Series, and they have been Japan's most famous and most popular team. The "Star" of the story is a boy named *Hoshi* (his name is a homonym for "star"). Hoshi's father tells him, "The only way to become a man and succeed in life is to suffer and persevere." Hoshi's father trains him so hard that the boy is reduced to a bleeding pulp, but he does grow up to be the star of the Giants. Ichiro's father says that his training of Ichiro was not like "Star of the Giants." Ichiro says it was.

The point is that the behavior of Hoshi's father was considered admirable. For Hoshi's father, as for Ichiro's, baseball is considerably more than a sport. As Robert Whiting, an English-speaking expert on baseball in Japan, explains, Japanese baseball has spiritual and philosophical meanings that run deep in the roots of Japanese culture and history. Like

Japanese martial arts, baseball is an activity that rewards those who cultivate "effort, fighting spirit, patience, and harmony." Ichiro's early training prepared him for the boot-camp-like atmosphere of Japanese high school ball and for the rigors of pro ball training camp. That is how Japanese players practice baseball. The reasons for this can be found in the history of baseball in Japan.

HOW BASEBALL CAME TO JAPAN

Baseball was still a new sport when it was brought to Japan in the 1870s. In 1853, Commodore Matthew Perry landed in Japan and ended the country's self-imposed isolation from the rest of the world, which began in the 1600s. Perry pried the country open with the threat of force, but the Japanese became fascinated with Western culture. The small feudal country embraced the Industrial Revolution. The Japanese brought in American and European teachers, advisors, and experts to revamp their sciences, military, transportation system, and industry. Through American university teachers, they were introduced to baseball—*bēsubōru* or *tama asobi* ("playing with a ball").

As early as the 1880s, however, there was also a Japanese *cultural* rejection of the West. They wanted to industrialize and to modernize—in some ways—but did not want to give up their own cultural values or traditions. In 1886, a school was created to teach and maintain Japanese values and traditions, called "First Higher School of Tokyo"—*Ichiko*. The students studied the martial arts and zen, but they also studied baseball. Maintaining tradition did not require the Japanese to reject the aspects of Western culture they found interesting but only to adapt them—to make them Japanese. So, they developed *seishin yakyū*—"spirit" or "spiritual" baseball. It was, as Robert Whiting explains, a way of turning baseball into something like a martial art. The school's version of the game came to

Baseball players from Waseda and Keio universities warmed up before a game in the 1930s. From its inception, baseball was more than just a sport in Japan—it was a discipline, a way to train the body, mind, and spirit of the player.

include 4 A.M. runs, even in the winter, and "1,000 swing" batting practices.

These hard practices were not just to produce winning teams. At some point in Japanese baseball history, the ideal game was a tie because no one "lost face"—suffered shame. Baseball was not so much a sport as a discipline, a physical and spiritual *practice*. That is not "practice" as in "we have to practice to get ready for the big game" or "I have to practice the piano." People who do yoga or meditation are "practitioners" of these activities. This is practice as a goal unto itself, a way of training the mind, body, and spirit all at the same time. In the case of "spiritual baseball," Whiting says, the goals were "strength, skill, stamina, courage, 'martial timing,' and an immovable mind." It is useful to remember this list while contemplating Ichiro's early training, as well as some of what he says later about his goals as a player.

Although Japanese Ichiko baseball was, in some ways, conceived as batter against pitcher, matching their skills and concentration against each other, it also fostered loyalty to the team and to the school and reflected the traditional Japanese value of cooperation and *Wa*, meaning group harmony or unity. It is more than "teamwork." No matter how big a star someone is, he can never forget that he is playing for the team, not for his own glory or stats.

There are, of course, Japanese athletes who have rebelled against the rigorous training or the emphasis on doing everything exactly as the coach says. Orestes Destrade (a Cuban American who played pro baseball in the United States and Japan) notes that modern Japanese Little Leaguers who have grown up watching Major League Baseball have been influenced by the American style. He says it used to be that "same is good." Now it is "different is good."

In 1896, the Ichiko team won a series of games against an American team from the Yokohama Country and Athletic Club. The Japanese team understood this as a victory of Japanese-style ball over American-style ball (which was still being played in the more Western schools in Japan). Japanese newspapers gave extensive coverage to the victory, further popularizing the Japanese "spiritual baseball" version of the game. Players cultivated their *konjō* ("fighting spirit") and *doryoku* ("effort"). Baseball's heroes were players like Tseunetaro Moriyama who, as part of his daily practice, threw a ball at a target on a brick wall until he wore a hole in the wall. He was also a great pitcher who gave up no runs to the

New York Yankees slugger Babe Ruth joined a handful of batboys at Kōshien Stadium in 1934 for a photo. Ruth and several other U.S. major leaguers toured Japan that year. The all-stars routinely defeated the amateur Japanese teams they faced, but the Japanese players still managed a highlight or two.

American team in 1896, but his greatness was not based on his statistics, it was based on his spirit and effort.

JAPANESE VERSUS U.S. BASEBALL GAMES

In 1905, a Japanese baseball team, from Waseda University, traveled to the United States for the first time. Although the Japanese team was beaten more often than not, it demonstrated a solid grasp of the game that impressed American spectators and newspaper reporters.

The Japanese team, Whiting says, picked up "pitchers' wind-ups, sacrifice bunts, sliding into base," as well as American-style cheering. Also, the team discovered more modern equipment. At the same time, the players came to value more than ever their style of play, their own spirit of the game. Their belief—which Ichiro agrees with—was that players grounded in a combination of American and Japanese baseball techniques would be able to defeat American players, despite the Americans' greater size and strength.

International play continued between the Japanese and the Americans. A University of Chicago team visited Japan in 1924 and lost a series to Waseda. In 1934, some major-league greats from the United States visited Japan. A team that included Babe Ruth and Lou Gehrig soundly defeated amateur Japanese teams, yet pitcher Eiji Sawamura struck out Ruth and Gehrig. Both Americans were cheered by Japanese fans and admired for their hitting prowess.

THE ARRIVAL OF PROFESSIONAL BASEBALL

In Yankee Stadium's left field during the 2006 season was a sign in Japanese and English that said "*Yomiuri.*" It is the name of Japan's biggest daily newspaper. In the 1930s, the Japanese were resisting the professionalization of baseball. They did not want the sport to be a job for pay but rather something done for its own sake. The owner of *Yomiuri*, Matsutaro Shoriki, sponsored the 1934 tour that brought Ruth and Gehrig to Japan, and he was inspired by the tour's success to create Japan's first professional baseball team. The team he started would become the Tokyo Giants—Japan's richest and most successful team. After the *Yomiuri* team toured the United States and met with considerable success against American teams (although not major-league teams), other companies started teams, eight in all. To this day, Japanese teams are still owned by companies and run more or less as advertisements for those companies.

The tough spirit of Japanese baseball carried into the new professional league—after the new *Yomiuri* team lost several games, manager Sadayoshi Fujimoto decided his team needed some discipline. He began what would be the Japanese pro ball tradition of all-day practices designed less to make better hitters or fielders of the players than, he said, to "hone their fighting spirit." They practiced until they bled, vomited, wept, or passed out cold. (They called it "vomit practice.") Although some teams were less strict, the Giants' training practices by and large became the standard for the pros. Then, as now, managers and players debated whether the long, hard practices made for better prepared and tougher teams or for teams that wore out early in the season (or players, early in their careers) from physical exhaustion or injuries.

WORLD WAR II

Just as Japanese pro baseball was getting established, World War II began. On December 7, 1941, Japan bombed the American naval base at Pearl Harbor in the U.S. territory of Hawaii. The bombing brought Japan and the United States into a war that had already engaged Germany, Great Britain, and Russia. Shortages of everything from transportation to wood to players limited baseball in the United States during the war. Still, the U.S. government believed that baseball was good for wartime morale, and the league and the country were big enough to cope with the difficulties. (Also, the major leagues began to get players from Latin American countries during this time.) Japan, however, is a smaller country, even if it has flourished despite an absence of natural resources like farmland and fuel. Its baseball league was small, too. The league was cut from eight teams to six and then shut down altogether.

Even before Japan bombed Pearl Harbor, the Japanese government had been preparing for war. By 1935, the Japanese Board of Education ruled that children must do "war calisthenics" rather than play baseball at school. When the war began, stadiums became ammunition dumps or were leveled. During the war, the language of baseball in Japan changed. Japan had mostly kept English terms for such things as strikes, balls, pitcher, and base. Now "out" became *hi-ké* (withdraw) and "safe" became *yoshi* (good). The Japanese fans had adored Babe Ruth and his home runs, but now Japanese soldiers yelled, "To hell with Beibu Rusu." Many Japanese players, including pitcher Eiji Sawamura, who had struck the Babe out, were killed in the war.

JAPAN REBUILDS

After the war, which ended in August 1945, General Douglas MacArthur and others in the U.S. military and government decided that, as the United States tried to help Japan rebuild, baseball could help people who had been enemies learn to work together. The Giants' stadium was turned back into a ballpark. A new stadium was built in the ruins of the city of Hiroshima, where the United States had dropped an atomic bomb. It would become the home field of the Hiroshima Toyo Carp. American servicemen played Japanese teams, and American major-league teams began to visit Japan again, as they had before the war. The Japanese professional league began to compete again, although the players had to grow their own food in order to be strong enough for the 1946 season. (During the war, most Japanese had to live on about one-third to one-half of the calories that people need to be healthy.)

In 1950, the Nippon Professional League (the equivalent of the American major leagues) split into the Central and the Pacific Leagues, their equivalent of the American and National Leagues. From the beginning, the Yomiuri Giants were the strongest team, and their league, the Central League, was the more popular league. (Ichiro would play in the Pacific League.) From 1959 to 1980, the Giants were the team of slugger

★ ★ ★ ★ ★
SADAHARU OH

Before the arrival of Hideo Nomo, Ichiro Suzuki, and in 2007, Daisuke Matsuzaka, perhaps the best-known Japanese baseball player in the United States was Sadaharu Oh, the acclaimed home-run hitter.

Oh, who was born in 1940, played first base for the Yomiuri Giants from 1959 to 1980. The team's hitting coach was an excellent swordsman, and Oh would practice sword slices to work on his batting swing. The results paid off. He won five Central League batting titles and led the league in home runs for 15 seasons. Oh hit 30 or more home runs in 19 straight seasons and holds the Japanese season record with 55 home runs. He finished his career with 868 home runs, more than Hank Aaron's major-league career record of 755. His team, the Giants, won 11 Japan Series titles, including nine in a row from 1964 to 1973.

After his playing days, he was the manager of the Yomiuri Giants for five seasons in the 1980s. He took over the reins of the Fukuoka Daiei Hawks of the Pacific League in 1995, leading the team to two wins in the Japan Series. In 2006, he was the manager of Japan's national team in the inaugural World Baseball Classic.

Oh's ballplaying prowess was not limited to his professional career. In 1957, he was the pitcher for his high school team in the Kōshien tournament. Blisters, from weeks of grueling practice, covered his hand as the team entered the final game. Blood dripped from his hand, his fingers were nearly numb, and still Oh pitched his team to victory.

Masanori Murakami, the first Japanese player in the major leagues, threw the ceremonial first pitch before a 2000 regular-season game between the New York Mets and Chicago Cubs at the Tokyo Dome in Japan. Murakami played with the San Francisco Giants in 1965, mostly as a relief pitcher, and had an ERA of 3.75. It would be 30 years before the next Japanese player appeared in the major leagues.

Sadaharu Oh, whose record of 868 career home runs is likely to stand for a while, if not forever.

Not only did major-league all-star teams travel to Japan during the off-season, but in 1951, a small number of Japanese players attended American spring training with the minor-league San Francisco Seals. In 1956, the Yankees became the first major-league team to have a scout in Japan. The great Casey Stengel said, "It may be four or five years, but I think the next great innovation in American baseball may be a Japanese star." The concerns then, though, were the same ones that Ichiro would face decades later: The Japanese players, however talented and well trained (and they were clearly both), were too small and not strong enough to play in the majors.

THE FIRST JAPANESE PLAYER IN THE MAJOR LEAGUES

In 1964, the Nankai Hawks sent three young players to play a season with a minor-league team of the San Francisco Giants. One of them was the left-handed pitcher Masanori Murakami. When Murakami was called up to the Giants for the following season, the Hawks said they wanted (and expected) him back. The Giants said that the $10,000 they had paid for each Japanese player's contract was binding. After a long, angry fight, a compromise was reached: Murakami would play for the Giants in 1965 and then decide where he wanted to play. During the 1965 season, he pitched 45 games (all but one in relief) and had a 3.75 earned-run average. He returned to his team in Japan, where he was, as it turned out, far less successful than he had been in the United States.

The door had been opened—Murakami was a popular and successful player—and then closed. The negotiations between the U.S. and Japanese teams over Murakami had left a bad taste in everyone's mouths. Retired or unsuccessful U.S. players continued to play on Japanese teams, and play between the two countries continued, but it would be many years before another Japanese player would sign a major-league contract in the United States. Japanese baseball contracts—and a cultural sense of duty to one's team—kept the Japanese players at home.

"Human Batting Machine"

Ichiro Suzuki did not know the city of Kobe, home of the Orix BlueWave, and he was not a special fan of any of the team's players—he was just glad to be in the pros. Years later, an interviewer asked him if he had had any doubts at the time whether he would be good enough to play Japanese professional ball. "People might get upset if I say this," he said, but he did not. It was not, however, entirely polite for him to say that he was that sure of himself.

ICHIRO IN THE JAPANESE MINOR LEAGUES

Ichiro may have been sure of himself, but Orix BlueWave manager Shozo Doi had doubts about his new player's ability. "You'll never make it, hitting that way," he said in disapproval, looking at Ichiro's nonstandard batting stance. In 1992, though, Ichiro—who at that time still had "Suzuki" on the back of his jersey—batted .366 in 58 games with the team's minor-league squad and .253 in 40 games with the BlueWave. Still, Doi sent him back down to the minors in 1993, telling him to work on that swing. In 1993, in the 43 games he played for the BlueWave, he hit only .188.

That did it. Ichiro was used to coaches and managers who believed that "a player has to know hardship if he's going to reach his full potential," as Doi said. By American standards, Ichiro had already suffered. Japanese pro teams play a shorter season than the American majors (140 games as of 2001, 130 when Ichiro began in 1992), but they train all day, from morning to night. After the season is over, they go right back to work. Ichiro practiced even longer, trying to get the new swing to work. Then, after hitting .188, he told Doi, "I've been hitting this way since high school. That's my batting. I'd rather stay on the farm than attempt a switch now." He could not bear to be playing that badly. Also, he disliked the idea of changing his batting style for a coach. Coaches would change over the years. "If I changed my style to suit a particular coach, then I'd lose sight of what sort of player I was and would fall apart completely. The worst possible pattern a professional player could fall into." It was rare for a young player, only two years out of high school, to say "no" to his manager, but Ichiro had been a baseball player for a long time and had developed his swing over a long time. He knew what felt right. So, back to the farm team he went.

Ichiro did not mind the minors. The farm-team manager, Kenichiro Kawamura, supported him and even argued with Doi about Ichiro. "You're killing everything that's good in him," Kawamura said. Doi believed that Ichiro played too easily, that he was succeeding too easily. That is what he meant by not suffering enough. Doi believed that, if Ichiro simply got better and better without knowing setbacks, he would be weaker spiritually. It is the same philosophy that led his father to tell coaches not to praise the young Ichiro. Later, Kawamura would say that he would have preferred to quit than to change Ichiro's swing. He said that Ichiro's form *looked* awkward but that he was, in fact, perfectly balanced. Kawamura worked with Ichiro on "the mental aspects of batting," for which Ichiro was grateful. Ichiro said that, while he had a feel for what worked, Kawamura "put that feeling into words. He'd say things like 'when you're trying to pick up the path of the ball coming toward you, pick it up first as a line, then as a point.'"

BECOMING "ICHIRO"

In 1994, the Orix BlueWave got a new manager. The team had done so badly under Doi that he resigned. The new manager, Akira Ogi, had been a second baseman for the Nishitetsu Lions, and he had been famous for his partying. Instead of telling the players they had to suffer, he said, "Drink hard, but practice hard." And his players did practice as hard as any others. Ogi did not care how Ichiro swung at the ball as long as he hit it. He moved Ichiro into the starting lineup and told him to go for it. Ichiro went for it: He hit .385 for the season and had 210 hits in 130 games, becoming the first Japanese player ever to have more than 200 hits in a season. He also stole 29 bases, had 54 RBIs, and safely reached base in 69 consecutive games, a Nippon Professional Baseball record. Playing center field, he won a Gold Glove, on top of being the Pacific League MVP, a "Best Nine" (like being an all-star) and an MSP (the Matsutaro Shoriki Prize, given since 1977 to a player or a manager who has contributed greatly to professional baseball in Japan). He donated his MVP money to nursing homes.

In 1994, Ichiro began to wear his first name on the back of his jersey. "Suzuki" is the second-most-common last name in Japan, and Ogi decided that it was time for his most distinguished player to be distinguished from the other Suzukis in the league. "Ichiro" is a common name, too, but no one was wearing it on the back of his baseball uniform. At first, Ichiro

Ichiro greeted Akira Ogi, his former Orix BlueWave manager, after Ogi threw out the first pitch in a game between the Seattle Mariners and the New York Yankees in August 2004. Ogi was the manager who first put Ichiro into the BlueWave's starting lineup. He was also the one who suggested that Ichiro wear only his first name on his jersey.

was embarrassed when announcers referred to him by his first name. It did, though, get the crowd's attention, which was what Ogi wanted. The BlueWave had not been doing very well, and the team was in the less-popular Pacific League. Ichiro's fans—and there were more of them all the time—loved calling him by his first name. Japanese fans are often very quiet, unless they are sitting in a section with professional cheerleaders, in which case they are very loud. (The cheerleaders use trumpets.) Ichiro's fans chanted his name and waved signs that said "Ichiro is Ichiban"—Ichiro is number one.

Ichiro was a little surprised at all the fuss he was creating. "There was a time when I felt the burden of everyone's expectations," he said. People had begun to wonder if he would be the first Japanese player to break .400. They compared him to the great home-run hitter Sadaharu Oh, not for his home runs, but for his bat speed. Endorsement offers poured in, and for the first time Ichiro was so popular that it was hard for him to take a quiet walk. His face was on everything from buttons and trading cards to towels and teacups.

THE KOBE EARTHQUAKE

The 1995 Nippon Professional Baseball season was played in the shadow of a tragedy. One night in January 1995, a loud noise awakened Ichiro, and he found that his room was swaying so much that he could not get out of bed. He was terrified that his dorm would collapse. His building did remain standing, but much of the city of Kobe did not. More than 6,000 people died in the quake and 300,000 people—about one-fifth of the city's population—were homeless. At first, Ichiro believed that the fans would have more important things to do than to watch baseball, but he was surprised and touched at how many people came out to support the team and, of course, to have their minds taken off their troubles.

Police officers and firefighters surveyed the damage of the collapsed Kobe-Osaka highway on January 18, 1995, a day after a major earthquake hit Kobe, Japan, killing more than 6,000 people. Ichiro and his team felt a responsibility to their fans and the city to help them heal after the devastation.

Ichiro and the whole BlueWave team felt a responsibility to their fans and to the city. As the city began its "Kobe comeback" campaign, team members wore patches on their sleeves that said *Gambarou Kobe*—"Let's do it for Kobe." Ichiro also donated considerable amounts of money to help people who had lost their homes.

HIDEO THE HERO

It was also in 1995 that pitcher Hideo Nomo changed the face of Japanese baseball. Aided by agent Don Nomura, Nomo figured out a way to break his contract with his team, the Kintetsu Buffaloes. Japanese players were, at that time, bound to their teams for an unbreakable 10-year period and, given the number of pitches thrown in a game (it could be 180 or 190 or even more), a pitcher could not count on a career much longer than that. Nomo, a well-paid, successful, and respected player, was 26 years old and several years away from free agency, and he had a great desire to play in the U.S. major leagues. Japanese players, though, did not do things like that. He was bound not only by his contract but also by *giri* and *on*—duty and obligation. Still, he felt very strongly that he needed to try. Japanese coaches believe that the best cure for a sore arm is to throw more pitches, but Nomo did not agree.

Nomo, Nomura, and an American agent, Arn Tellem, succeeded in finding a loophole in the standard Japanese baseball contract. The contract bound the player, even a retired player, to his team *as long as he stayed in Japan.* That wording prevented a player from announcing his retirement in order to sign with a different Japanese team. Nomo, though, did not want to stay in Japan, and that same wording meant that, once he announced his retirement, he was legally free to sign with an American team—an event no one had considered when the contracts were drawn up. So Nomo announced his retirement and signed with the Los Angeles Dodgers.

The outcry in Japan was immediate and loud. The press, representatives from Nippon Professional Baseball, and Nomo's own father told Nomo that he was a troublemaker and a traitor and was failing to show proper respect to his team and to his country. Essential to the game of baseball (as to everything in Japanese culture) is the notion of harmony and unity, and Nomo was turning his back on *wa* (team harmony) in a big way. "The Shame of Japan" he was called in one headline.

Nevertheless, Nomo went to the Dodgers and succeeded there. People began to point out that "Hideo" meant "hero." He became exceedingly popular in Japan, and every game in which he pitched was broadcast live in Japan. One TV station ran an 11-hour-long special on him.

Although Nippon Professional Baseball soon closed up what came to be known as the "Nomo clause" (without telling U.S. baseball officials), Nomo was followed by others, including Hideki Irabu (who went to the New York Yankees). It would not be until December 1998 that Major League Baseball and Nippon Professional Baseball hammered out an agreement that created a (relatively) smooth path from Japanese pro ball to U.S. pro ball. Still, Nomo succeeded in the United States and made it possible for other pitchers to do the same.

ICHIRO AND THE MAJOR LEAGUES

When Nomo went to the Dodgers, Ichiro was a young player and many years from free agency, but people speculated about whether his hitting was good enough for the major leagues. They tended to conclude, as they always had, that Japanese batters would not be able to hit American pitchers. Ichiro thought otherwise. "As long as the ball is thrown by a human being, I have the confidence to hit any pitch, no matter how fast it comes," he said. Then, with the courtesy, humility, and loyalty to his team that were expected of him, he added, "But I never thought of playing in the major leagues. . . . If I did, I'd probably hit only .250."

Still, when Ichiro was a child dreaming of signing a pro contract, playing for the major leagues was not a possibility. Now it was.

The 1995 season was another great one for Ichiro. Although he would not again achieve 200 hits in the regular season in Japan, he finished the season with a .342 batting average, the best in the league. He had 25 home runs, 80 RBIs, and 49 stolen bases. He led the league in hits (179), RBIs, and stolen bases. He never led in walks (he hates to walk). The press called him "The Human Batting Machine."

Ichiro also inspired his team. Excited by his performance and spurred on by their desire to encourage their damaged city, the BlueWave led the Pacific League for the first time. The team went on to play in the Japan Series, in which it was defeated by the Yakult Swallows of the Central League.

WINNING THE JAPAN SERIES

Ichiro's father was still very much on the scene. As often as he could, he made the two-hour drive to watch the BlueWave's home games in Kobe. He published a book that he would later revise and republish as *Musuko Ichiro* ("My Son, Ichiro"). During games, Mr. Suzuki would sit on the infield bleachers, signing autographs and talking to reporters. After his embarrassed son asked him to stop, Mr. Suzuki sat in the outfield seats.

In 1996, the BlueWave not only won the Pacific League pennant but also defeated the Yomiuri Giants to win the Japan Series. The Giants' roster included that year's Central League MVP, a left fielder named Hideki Matsui.

After the 1996 season, Ichiro played exhibition games on a Japanese all-star team against a visiting team of major-league all-stars, including Cal Ripkin, Jr., Barry Bonds, Pedro Martínez, Alex Rodriguez, and Mike Piazza. It was not the first time that Ichiro had played against American players (many play in Nippon Professional Baseball), and it was not the first time the major league had seen Ichiro's stuff. Baseball manager Bobby Valentine, who managed the 1995 Chiba Lotte Marines and managed the New York Mets from 1996 to 2002, had seen Ichiro play and said he was "one of the five best players in the world." Still, the major-league players and Ichiro got a good look at one another during that series. The great hitter Mike Piazza said that Ichiro was good enough to play in the majors. When Ichiro heard that, he modestly said, "I could go, but I would probably be the bat boy."

In fact, he considered himself bound both by his contract and by *on* and *giri* (obligation and duty). He owed his team and

Ichiro blasted a home run in the top of the tenth inning to lead the Orix BlueWave to a 4-3 victory over the Yomiuri Giants in the first game of the 1996 Japan Series. The BlueWave won the Japan Series, and after the season, Ichiro played in several exhibition games against U.S. major leaguers.

his manager his loyalty and his services, and he was—despite the portrayal of him in the Japanese media as young, modern, and hip-hop—in many ways traditional in his beliefs. After Ichiro's 1996 season, the BlueWave management offered him a one-year contract worth 260 million yen (more than $2 million), rather than the much higher amount many people had predicted. Ichiro signed. (Japanese baseball players were not allowed to have agents until 2000. It was up to the player and his team to agree on the contract.) He told a newspaper reporter, "I have actually only been playing professional baseball for three years. I wonder how it would appear if I had asked for the same kind of money that the top guys are making."

Still, Ichiro would be a free agent in 2001 and, after the 1996 Japan–U.S. series, he began to think about the majors in a different way. "Instead of just something I admired from afar, the majors became a goal of mine," he later told an interviewer. He had watched major-league pitchers on television, but in 1996 he had actually batted against them, and he had hit .636—7 hits in 11 at-bats, with 2 stolen bases.

THE NOT VERY PRIVATE LIFE OF ICHIRO

Ichiro was so famous that mail addressed to "Ichiro/Japan" would be delivered to him. Endorsements had been rolling in, followed by his own product lines. By 1997, a line of clothing bore his name and rapidly became one of the best-selling brands in Japan. The Japanese are enthusiastic fans (the sort who remind us that the word *fan* is short for *fanatic*), and Ichiro found himself with very little privacy. When he traveled with the team, typically by bullet train, he could not sleep: Fans would wake him up to get his autograph. When he traveled by car, he could not stop at public restrooms: Whoever was next to him at the urinal would yell, "It's Ichiro! It's Ichiro!"—and there he would be, mobbed by strangers while he was trying to go to the bathroom.

Ichiro did not fight fame. On the field, he hotdogged for the crowds, throwing the ball all the way to left field from right during warm-ups and playing catch with people in the stadium. Once, during a delay, he went to the pitcher's mound and threw some pitches. When he puts on his uniform, he is *Ichiro*, and he believes he has responsibilities to the people who have come to see him. They deserve, he believes, the best baseball he can play and some entertainment, too.

At the same time, the way Ichiro dressed—baggy pants, a backward or sideways baseball cap, and custom-made sneakers for casual wear and very expensive Japanese-made suits for formal occasions—was for himself, not for his fans. With his taste for hip-hop music, trendy, expensive sunglasses, and fashionable clothes, Ichiro seemed to be what the press said he was, the "modern face of Japan." His interests, though, were golf (which he could not play in Japan because the caddies all wanted his autograph), growing *bonsai* trees (an ancient Japanese art), and playing *Go* (an ancient Japanese board game). He loved his dog and his tropical fish, which he could stare at for hours to rest his eyes and mind. They are, as one magazine pointed out, the hobbies of an old man. Ichiro would have liked to have kept those selves separate, to be the famous baseball player in uniform and a quiet, thoughtful man with a taste for modern music and old-fashioned hobbies in private. He was not allowed to.

It became nearly impossible for him to see the woman he was dating, sportscaster Yumiko Fukushima. They started going out in 1997 after she interviewed him, and by October 1998, Ichiro went to Yumiko's parents to say that they were seeing each other and planned to marry.

Their reasons for wanting to be together were ordinary ones. They loved each other, and both said they felt completely comfortable together. Their dates, though, were not ordinary. To eat out, they had to reserve a private room at a restaurant and post guards at the door. Once, his teammates rolled Ichiro in a carpet and smuggled him out of the dorm in the back of a truck to get him to a date. It makes a funny story, but for a 25-year-old man and a professional 32-year-old woman, it was not all that amusing.

SECRET WEDDING

Ichiro and Yumiko married on December 3, 1999, at a country club in Los Angeles, California. Only a few friends and their families joined them. They flew separately, under fake names, to dodge the press. Still, Ichiro says, it was a beautiful wedding, planned mostly by their friends. When the ceremony was over and the marriage vows were exchanged, Ichiro surprised everyone by starting to cry. He surprised himself, too, but said that joy and gratitude overwhelmed him.

The well-traveled and poised Yumiko seemed a wise choice for Ichiro. He does not like to speak about his private life, but he does say how grateful he is to her and how much he appreciates her strength and support. It is hard to be the wife of a baseball player. Baseball players travel and they worry (slumps, contracts), and Ichiro would travel farther and worry more than most. Yumiko was modern and independent enough to help him cope with their eventual move to the United States, but she was also willing to make a traditional Japanese home for him, pack his lunch, and take over the housekeeping. (Ichiro was known for being a neat freak when he was single—he ironed his own T-shirts—though Yumiko says he never picked up a sock after they were married.) Whether she was able to distract him from his 24-hour-a-day obsession with baseball is open to debate. Although they do not talk about baseball much, Ichiro never entirely stops training. Even while sleeping he trains, rolling from side to side because sleeping with all his weight on one arm will cause his body to "get out of balance." Yumiko is responsible for his beard: She told him it would make him look like Brad Pitt.

THE DARK SIDE

By 1998, the BlueWave was struggling. The team was not playing as well as it had been, and it was not attracting fans the same way either. The team was in the less-popular league, and most of its games were not televised. In 1998, Ichiro again won the batting title and led the league in hits, but he stole only 11 bases. He was bored.

He was also terribly unhappy with his level of play, and he had been since 1995. "People kept praising me, saying how great my batting was, but, believe me, over and over I felt like I was thrown into the pits of despair. . . . During the seven years I played for Orix, I often felt lost and, deep down, never really

★ ★ ★ ★ ★ ☆

ICHIRO'S BLUEWAVE HIGHLIGHTS

In his first full season with the Orix BlueWave, Ichiro set a Japanese pro-ball record with 210 hits for the season. Ichiro has said that he was often unhappy with his play during his years with the BlueWave. Yet, the hits record was just one of many set by Ichiro during his Japanese playing career. Here are a few of his accomplishments:

- Winner of the batting title in all seven seasons, tying a record for most batting championships.
- Winner of a Gold Glove and named as a "Best Nine" (all-star) in all seven seasons.
- A career batting average of .353, the highest among Nippon Professional Baseball players with at least 2,000 at-bats.
- Named Most Valuable Player three years in a row, 1994 to 1996.
- Reached base in a record 69 consecutive games during the 1994 season.
- Went 216 consecutive at-bats without a strikeout during the 1997 season.
- Was hit by a pitch 18 times in the 1995 season, then a record.

believed in my abilities as a ballplayer." He was angry at himself all the time, except in 1994.

This is, perhaps, the dark side of Ichiro's insistence that he be the judge of his own performance. He resists getting caught up in statistics, streaks, and awards. He believes that a player who pays too much attention to these external notions becomes too vulnerable to what other people think and loses sight of himself and his goals. When asked to comment on his awards or records, he often uses a phrase that is translated as, "I don't want to rest on my laurels." This quest to continually improve has shaped Ichiro's life and his career, but it also means that he cannot be comforted by what others say of him or by his great statistics. Ichiro says that his unhappiness during those difficult years with the BlueWave was not just "psychological turmoil or depression" but was based on a genuine inability to get comfortable with some technical aspects of hitting. It certainly sounds, though, like psychological turmoil. Like many baseball players, he can get caught up in the minutiae—the tiny details—of hitting. It is the sort of self-analysis that can help a player grow but can also become a kind of self-torture.

SECURE IN HIS BATTING

In 1999, Ichiro had a breakthrough in his hitting. He started the season in a slump, hitting .213. He said he could not visually pick up the ball as it came toward him. Then, in an April 11 game against the Seibu Lions, he grounded out. "The worst kind of grounder," he says—yet suddenly "a mist cleared up before my eyes." He felt everything fall into place—eyes, stance, timing. After that Ichiro enjoyed batting more than he had for a long time. Even if he hit badly, he felt secure, believing he had the tools and the ability to figure out what was wrong and fix it. During the 1999 season, his batting average was between .375 and .400. No Japanese player had yet hit .400 for a season, but it seemed Ichiro might. His control was, at times, uncanny, as on May 13, 2000, when he was able to hit a ball that had bounced in front of the plate.

Ichiro suffered injuries at the end of 1999 and 2000 and so did not play a full season either year. The 1999 injury—a broken wrist after being hit by a pitch—ended a 763-consecutive-game streak and prevented him from playing for almost five months. It also made it difficult for him to brush his teeth or hold chopsticks, but it gave him time to see friends, go to concerts, and walk around the city. In August 2000, Ichiro pulled a muscle in his side and then went running because he had missed his workout that day (he feels bad if he goes a whole day without working out). A run, with an injury, in the mountains of Kobe took Ichiro out of the lineup for the rest of the season.

After the 1999 season, Ichiro's motivation for wanting to get into the major leagues changed. Before then, he thought of it as a challenge but mostly as a way out of his unhappiness. Once he regained confidence in his hitting, the major leagues seemed to be the place to test his skill "at the highest level of baseball in the world." Additionally, the Orix fans had gotten used to Ichiro's abilities. Attendance had been dropping since the 1996 Japan Series win. "If I'd been hitting .450 or .500, with 50 home runs, maybe a few fans would have come," he said later, obviously exaggerating. But if people did not want to see him play ball, which is what he wants to offer people, and they wanted to disturb his private life, which he dislikes, then what did he have left to give people?

MAJOR LEAGUES (PART ONE)

The Orix BlueWave management knew that Ichiro wanted to play in the major leagues because he had said so, beginning in 1996. BlueWave scout Katsutoshi Miwata laughed. Ichiro trusted Miwata and figured it was too soon. In August 1999, manager Ogi invited Ichiro to dinner and said that he needed Ichiro on the team and would not release him. Ogi had

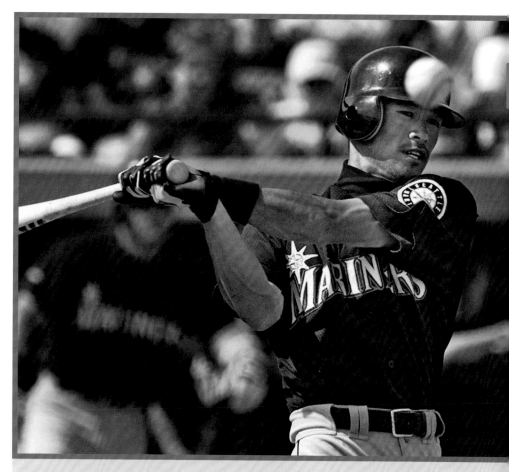

In 1999, Ichiro was able to spend spring training with the Seattle Mariners in Peoria, Arizona. Here, he fouls off a ball in a game. Ichiro was getting the itch to make the move to Major League Baseball.

supported Ichiro from the beginning, by bringing him up from the minors and not trying to change his batting stance. Aside from the bonds of duty and obligation, Ichiro also owed an individual debt to this man. If Ogi was not going to let him go with a blessing, then Ichiro was not going to the majors. He would wait until his contract was up in 2001.

Although Ogi had said that Ichiro could not go to the majors, Ogi did send him (and two teammates) in 1999 for two

weeks of spring training and some exhibition games with the Seattle Mariners in Peoria, Arizona. The Mariners are owned in part by the Japanese owner of Nintendo. For Ichiro, the trip was another chance to test himself against American major-league pitchers. He asked Mariner teammate Jamie Moyer, "Can I play in the U.S.?"—meaning "Am I good enough?" The Americans knew he was fast and had a good arm. What no one could tell was how his hitting would hold up over a 162-game season. During his time there, though, Ichiro got sick and missed some exhibition games.

MAJOR LEAGUES (PART TWO)

After strong 1999 and 2000 seasons, Ichiro had one more year left on his contract with the BlueWave. The team's management had a choice: It could keep Ichiro for one more year. Then he would try to leave for the majors. Ichiro was an expensive player, now earning about $5 million a year. His new salary would be higher. The alternative was to use the new "posting" system that had been put in place between Major League Baseball and Nippon Professional Baseball.

According to the posting system, the Japanese team can announce which of its players under contract are available. U.S. teams interested in that player submit sealed bids to the player's Japanese team. The U.S. team that offers the most money (above an undisclosed minimum that the Japanese team has established) wins the right to negotiate with the player. No other team can negotiate with the player, and if he and the major-league team fail to come to an agreement within 30 days, then the Japanese team keeps the player.

The BlueWave decided to "post" Ichiro. There was a certain amount of scrambling in the majors at this point. Teams had to guess how much money the BlueWave would accept for Ichiro and guess what competing teams would offer. Ichiro's agent, Tony Attanasio, said that only teams from cities with a strong

Asian presence should bid. The Seattle Mariners were an obvious choice. The team had Japanese ownership and a Japanese pitcher, Kazuhiro Sasaki, who had just won Rookie of the Year. Ichiro had gone to their spring training. Bobby Valentine, who was then the manager of the Mets, wanted Ichiro, too. So did some other teams. In the end, the Mariners' bid of $13,125,000 won them the right to negotiate with Ichiro. Twenty hours of negotiations with Attanasio produced a contract that was acceptable to everyone. It was a three-year, $14 million contract that included English lessons and an interpreter.

Ichiro's father had said that he should wait until he was a free agent, but he then said (in Japanese), "Go for it." His mother had worried if he would eat right but was convinced by Yumiko that her boy would not starve. The contract was a great relief to Ichiro. He had spent time with the Mariners and he knew and liked Sasaki, whom he had played against in Japan. He had done it: He was going to the majors.

Ichiro wore a Mariners cap around the house in Kobe, smiling like a child.

The Wizard: Rookie Year with the Mariners

On November 9, 2000, the Seattle Mariners signed Ichiro Suzuki, the first Japanese position player to come to Major League Baseball in the United States. He was believed to be Japan's best player, but he was almost unknown in the United States.

The Mariners needed Ichiro. The team was founded in 1976, but it had mostly been an embarrassment until the mid-1990s. Seattle made baseball history in 1986 when Roger Clemens struck out 20 Mariners in one nine-inning game. (It was a major-league record but not the kind teams hope to achieve.) After the 1992 season, the team hired manager Lou Piniella. On the Mariners' roster were Ken Griffey, Jr., pitcher Randy Johnson, designated hitter Edgar Martinez, and outfielder Jay Buhner. Alex Rodriguez and pitcher Jamie Moyer

More than 90 members of the media, most of them from Japan, gathered for Ichiro's first appearance in Seattle on November 30, 2000, just a few weeks after he signed a three-year contract with the Seattle Mariners. The media throng would be a nuisance to Ichiro, and others, during his rookie season. "How many times can they watch me stretch?" Ichiro said.

both joined the team in 1996. The Mariners won the American League West in 1995 and 1997 and got a new stadium—Safeco Field—in 1999, after the old one began to fall down.

The team traded Johnson in the middle of 1998. (When Ichiro inherited Johnson's number, 51, he promised Johnson he would not bring shame to it.) Griffey was traded at the end of 1999, and Rodriguez, as a free agent, left for Texas after the 2000 season, earning the most expensive contract in baseball history. And the Mariners were signing a Japanese player most American fans had never heard of and Bret Boone, part of the third generation of the Boone dynasty to play in the major leagues. No one knew how the Mariners would fare without

☆ ☆ ☆ ☆ ☆

JAPAN AND THE MARINERS' HISTORY

The Seattle Mariners team, which played its first game in 1977, was created because of a lawsuit. Bud Selig (who would become the commissioner of baseball in the 1990s) bought the Seattle Pilots and moved them to Milwaukee in 1971. The city of Seattle and the state of Washington sued the American League for breach of contract. They had a stadium and were supposed to have a team, they said. The lawsuit sought $32 million in damages, but in 1976 the city agreed to take a new expansion team instead.

In 1991, Seattle almost lost its team again. The Mariners seldom won, and few fans came to see them, so the owner threatened to move the team to Florida. The chief executive officer of Nintendo, Hiroshi Yamauchi, offered to buy the team as a present for Seattle. (He lived in Japan and does not even watch baseball, but the company's American headquarters is in Seattle.) The owner of the Philadelphia Phillies (and polls taken across the their great pitcher and famous sluggers, and no one knew how the small, slender Japanese star would hit against major-league pitchers. Piniella said he would be satisfied if Ichiro hit .270 or .280.

WELCOME NO. 51

Certainly Ichiro felt welcomed. Japanese baseball had said good-bye and thank you with a ceremony that brought him nearly to tears. (He said he wished they had chosen more cheerful music.) The Mariners welcomed him to Safeco Field with "Ichiro Day," fireworks, and a giant turnout from the media. (They had done the same for Kazuhiro Sasaki the year

☆ ☆ ☆ ☆ ☆ ☆

United States) said that it was not "patriotic" to have a Japanese owner of an American team. The commissioner of baseball (then Fay Vincent) agreed. The city of Seattle did not. The city had Japanese companies and Japanese citizens and did not mind having a Japanese owner of its baseball team. In 1992, a compromise was reached: Yamauchi would buy 60 percent of the team, but his voting interest would be restricted to 49 percent. (This limit was lifted in 1996.) Fay Vincent has since said that he is not proud of his original opposition.

According to Howard Lincoln, the Mariners' chief executive officer and the former chairman of Nintendo of America, Yamauchi is the reason that Ichiro is playing in Seattle—he knew enough about marketing to suggest that the team pursue Ichiro when he became available. "I don't think any one of us Americans at the Mariners really understood the impact this one guy could have," Lincoln said in an interview with *Business Week* magazine.

before.) To Ichiro, the whole situation seemed almost unreal, as if he were in a movie.

A number of players and coaches had seen Ichiro before, during spring training in 1999 and, of course, 2001. Some had played against him in Japan, during the all-star exhibition games. Oakland manager Art Howe, for instance, played against Ichiro in 1998. "What I saw was an outfielder who could fly, a guy with a great arm and a terrific natural hitter. I knew we were in trouble when I saw him steal second against Pudge [Texas catcher Iván Rodríguez]. And it wasn't even close."

Ichiro and Yumiko Suzuki faced changes in language, culture, food, and every other aspect of daily life. Before spring training, they stayed in a hotel in Seattle until they found an apartment with three bedrooms—so that Ichiro could have a room in which to practice his swings. Yumiko Suzuki was the one to face many of the daily challenges of life in a new country. She spoke some English and took care of the house. Although Seattle has a large Japanese community, ordinary activities like food shopping were harder there. She found it difficult to get meat and fish that were as fresh as in Japan. Some things became easier over time, of course, The Suzukis' local grocery store began to order some of Ichiro's favorite brands of food and snacks, including Pocari Sweat Drink, BlackBlack chewing gum, and Boss coffee.

MAJOR-LEAGUE VERSUS JAPANESE PRO BALL

Ichiro had to adjust to a number of differences between the Japanese game and American major-league baseball. People had questioned if a Japanese position player could ever succeed against bigger, stronger American pitchers. They had wondered about a Japanese player getting used to the bigger strike zone (it is wider on the outside). The season is longer, and so are the road trips. Games can be longer: A Japanese pro game only can go as long as 12 innings to break a tie; then the game is called a draw and everyone goes home.

In addition, there were many other adjustments for a Japanese player to make. Most American fields have natural grass while most Japanese fields have Astroturf. (The different surfaces affect how the ball bounces, Ichiro says, and players can run flat out on real grass but not on artificial turf.) American fields are all different. Most are asymmetrical and have a great deal of variation in how deep they are in the outfield and in the amount of space between the foul line and the bleachers. In Japan, the fields are symmetrical and alike. Ichiro would have to get used to defending different sizes and shapes of right field. (He would report that the variations of American fields made them interesting to play in but that he was glad for the padding on most outfield walls, also new to him.) The baseball itself is different. A Japanese pro baseball is slightly smaller and softer. At first, Ichiro found the American ball too dry and slippery, and its stitching too rough. Even the fans are different. American fans sit closer to the field and are not separated from the field by screens. They yell more, too, and, Ichiro would say later, follow the game more closely.

And, of course, there were all the cultural differences in philosophies toward the game and training habits. The Americans had a shorter spring training, no fall training or practice on game days, and no drills like the ones Ichiro was used to at home. American players did not help rake the field or even care for their own equipment.

ICHIRO ADJUSTS

Observers of baseball who thought that Ichiro would have trouble adjusting to major-league pitching or the larger strike zone had underestimated Ichiro's professionalism, intelligence, and attention to detail. Sometimes what he does looks like pure brilliance, but it is the brilliance of someone who knows how to pay attention and leaves little to chance. Ichiro had been preparing himself for the major-league strike zone since 1996. During practices he would sometimes ask the BlueWave catcher, a Major League Baseball fan, if each pitch would have been a major-league strike. In 2000, he sometimes played with an imaginary major-league strike zone. "I'd make my personal strike zone bigger," he said.

Ichiro had also started to adjust his swing after visiting the Mariners' spring-training camp in 1999, using less of a front-leg lift. He made further changes during spring training in 2001 to adjust to the differences in American and Japanese pitching. The Japanese pitcher's rhythm is something like "1, 2, and (pause) 3," and Ichiro's unusual front-leg lift was on the "and." The pause is when the Japanese pitchers gather their strength (say Japanese players) or try to deceive the batter (say American commentators). Whatever its explanation, it does not exist in American pitching, and Ichiro had to get used to not having that pause. Although he had been studying videos of major-league pitching and the leg lift was already lower than it had been, he eliminated it during spring training.

During spring training, manager Lou Piniella became worried about Ichiro's tendency to hit everything to left field. He did not seem to be able to pull the ball. Sportswriters noticed it, too. Ichiro says he was preparing himself for the season in his own way. Part of his tendency to hit to left field was caused by his having to adjust to the wider strike zone. He was focusing on outside pitches. Additionally, he would tell interviewer Narumi Komatsu, he was still involved in building an invisible "wall" on the right side of his body, something he does at the beginning of each season. "In order to strengthen this wall in the beginning I have to be more conscious of the area left of center. Not that I couldn't pull a ball to the right all of a sudden, but if I do that my wall breaks down."

Still, Piniella was concerned, and Ichiro believes that while it is his job to get ready for the season, he also has a responsibility to give confidence to his manager, coaches, and teammates. His preparation complete, he began to spray hits all around the field, including some home runs. At this point, Piniella, the press, Ichiro's teammates, and some of his opponents began to get a feel for Ichiro's ability to hit the ball where he wanted. People would continue to comment on this ability with increasing degrees of wonder, awe, and disbelief as the season progressed. As Al Martin, a Mariners outfielder, said, "Nobody is that good. This isn't Little League. You don't just walk into your first spring training, hang around, and set people up." Center fielder Mike Cameron said, "It's like he's playing T-ball out there. He hits wherever he wants to whenever he wants to."

Ichiro's teammates found him exhilarating. He was completely professional but obviously thrilled to be in the majors. The stretches, squats, and calisthenics he did amazed them. Most of them could not have done those moves without tearing a hamstring. Ichiro tried to fit in. He did not know much English, but he would greet teammates with "Wassup?" and "Thanks, dawg," which he had learned from his hip-hop music. His teammates added some four-letter curse words to his vocabulary, and teased him. He played along and, later in the season, cheerfully participated in the annual hazing that Mariner rookies undergo, which involves having their clothes stolen from their locker and replaced by others—in Ichiro's case, the short skirt and tight shirt of a Hooters waitress. (The clothes are now in the Ichiro museum.)

Ichiro's teammates soon called him "Wizard" for his amazing abilities. Ichiro, encouraged by Sasaki, began to eat American food sometimes, but Bret Boone, the team's other new player, would soon be eating Japanese rice balls for lunch every day, packed for him by Yumiko Suzuki. The day Boone first tried rice balls with pickled plum inside, he hit a home run, so he decided rice balls were good luck.

THE PRESS

Another question for the Mariners, aside from how well their new rookie would do, was what to do with all the press. The

Mariners had never seen anything like it. One writer counted 97 members of the media present on the first day of spring training, 85 of them from Japan. Ichiro was mobbed, surrounded by a sea of microphones, cameras, and reporters yelling questions. The people around him felt the media invasion, too. "I threw Ichiro a lot of batting practice early," said John McLaren, the Mariners' bench coach. "One day they came up to me and said, 'Yesterday, Ichiro took 214 swings. Today, he took 196. What's wrong?'" McLaren was flabbergasted. He does not count batting-practice swings, and he had never been asked a question like that in his life.

Ichiro, who was used to the Japanese press but tired of them, began to sound a little annoyed. "How many times can they watch me stretch? How many times can they watch me take batting practice? They are always there." He added later, "I understand everyone has a job to do. But don't you think they could just take a little break?"

They could not. The Japanese reporters had to write, or film, something about Ichiro every day. He was Japan's best player, and if he could not make it in the majors, no one could. His presence in the majors was so important to the Japanese that Japanese television funded a yearlong documentary about Ichiro's rookie year. Brad Lefton, a Japanese-speaking American TV producer, recorded Ichiro's entire first year in the United States to create the documentary.

Ichiro knew what his being in the majors meant to people. How could he not know, when everyone spoke of it so much? Piniella said, "He's like Lewis and Clark. I don't think Ichiro knows who Lewis and Clark were, though."

Ichiro himself said:

Obviously, I am the first position player to come over. People say I am an explorer, a pioneer, whatever. [But] that's not why I came over here. I came over here to play baseball.

I don't play baseball for other people. I play baseball for myself. . . . I just play the best I can.

Yet he also knew he was playing for two countries. The first exhibition game of the season, against the San Diego Padres, was shown live on television in Japan—at five in the morning. His BlueWave games had not even been televised and the stadiums had not been full, but now that he was on the Mariners, Japanese baseball fans were getting up at dawn to watch him.

OPENING DAY

On April 2, Ichiro made his major-league debut in the first game of the regular season, at home, against the Oakland A's. Piniella considered having Ichiro bat third but put him in as the leadoff hitter because of his incredible speed to first base—3.7 or 3.8 seconds. He ran quickly, but he also got out of the batter's box so fast that he seemed to be running before he had even finished hitting.

Safeco Field was sold out. The crowd was the largest one ever for a regular-season game, and it included many Japanese fans who had flown in to see Ichiro's first game, including Ichiro's father. It was also broadcast on Japanese radio and by two TV stations. An estimated 12 million fans were watching or listening in Japan when the game began at 11:15 A.M. Japanese time. "A lot of Japanese baseball fans took an early lunch today," one reporter said.

Ichiro did not get a hit in his first three at-bats. Then, in the seventh inning, with the Mariners behind by two runs, Ichiro got his first hit off pitcher T. J. Mathews, a grounder to center field. The game came to a temporary halt while the crowd cheered, and Ichiro called for a time-out to ask for the baseball. Edgar Martinez's hit sent Ichiro home. When Ichiro came to the plate in the eighth, the score was tied and Carlos Guillén was on first with a walk. Oakland's infield was playing deep, looking for

On Opening Day 2001, Ichiro sprinted down the first-base line to beat the throw after bunting in the eighth inning against the Oakland Athletics. The hit was his second of the day and contributed to the Mariners' 5-4 victory.

characteristically, he hit a 100-mile-per-hour (161-kilometer-per-hour) fastball thrown by Randy Johnson, the 6-foot-10-inch (208-centimeter) former Mariner.

MORE PRESS

The downside of Ichiro's growing fame was the increasing intensity of the press coverage. According to rumors, a Japanese magazine had offered $1 million for a photo of Ichiro without any clothes. (To this day, he showers and dresses in private.) Teammate Al Martin suggested that he take the picture and they split the money. Asked how much money he wanted for a posed nude shot, Ichiro said, "I'd do it if they'd disappear." Did that mean if the press would stop following him? "I'd do it if they'd disappear from the planet." After cameramen blocked Ichiro's car as he tried to back out of his garage, and other incidents, Ichiro and Sasaki boycotted the Japanese press for a week. During this period, Ichiro went 0-for-21, hitless for four games in a row. The Mariners' management dealt with this by limiting the media's access to Ichiro to brief press conferences at the end of each game. Ichiro and Sasaki ended the boycott. Ichiro hit in 34 of his next 35 games and batted .429 for the month of August. On August 28, he was the first major-league player to get 200 hits for the season.

SEPTEMBER 11

By early September, the Mariners were on their way toward winning the American League West. Then on September 11, terrorists in hijacked airliners brought down the Twin Towers of the World Trade Center in New York City and destroyed part of the Pentagon outside Washington, D.C. All major-league play was halted.

Ichiro and Yumiko Suzuki were in Anaheim, California. The Mariners were expected to clinch the division title during that series with the Angels, so many of the players' wives were there. Ichiro and Yumiko were relieved to be together, but Ichiro said later that, for the rest of his life, he would remember the shock he felt when he saw the World Trade Center towers on television. When the series resumed a week later, the meaning of the games had changed for him. The game was not about the pennant race anymore. "It meant something far more significant: that baseball had returned to America," he said.

On September 19, when the Mariners clinched the division, the players wore American flags on their uniforms. As in Kobe after the earthquake, Ichiro at first questioned if this was a time to be playing baseball. As in Kobe, he realized how important it was that the season continue. For fans, doing something as normal and ordinary as watching a baseball game was helpful as people tried to get on with their lives.

The division title was the Mariners' first in four years, and they did it by tying the all-time record for wins in a season: 116 wins and 46 losses. On September 29, Ichiro got his 234th hit, breaking Shoeless Joe Jackson's 1911 record for the most hits by a rookie. Ichiro ended the regular season as the top batter (.350) and top base stealer (56) in the American League. He was surprised. He had known in midseason that he had one of the top three batting averages, and he had wondered when he would fall off the list. Instead, the averages of other players fell, and Ichiro came out on top. He had tried not to think about it. He said later, "From past experiences I know that if I start to really want a title I get too self-conscious and my body gets out of synch." Also, he said, "If you start wanting it too much you get too concerned about other people. The one thing I can't stand is hoping that other people will mess up." For Ichiro, what he has accomplished is always of less concern than what he will do next. "To me, what I have done is not important. To me what is important is how I prepare for the game every day."

A dejected Ichiro sat in the dugout on October 22, 2001, after the Mariners lost the American League Championship Series to the New York Yankees. Ichiro, though, had had a stellar rookie season. He was named the American League Rookie of the Year and the Most Valuable Player—the first time in more than 25 years that the same player received both awards.

THE POSTSEASON

The Mariners faced the Cleveland Indians, the Central Division champions, in a best-of-five series. The Mariners needed all five games to win the series, but they did—with Ichiro hitting

.600 for the five games. They then had to play the Yankees for the American League pennant and the chance to play in the World Series.

Although the Mariners had more wins in the season than the Yankees, the Yankees had won the last three World Series. It was a strong year for a strong franchise. Additionally, the Yankees were trying to bolster the morale of the city of New York after the September 11 attacks. Each Yankee seemed to be playing slightly better than usual, and, for baseball fans, the heroic efforts of the Yankees seemed one of the only normal things left in the city. Not even Ichiro could hit the Yankee pitching in that pennant race, and the Mariners won only one game against them. The exhausted Yankees went on to lose the World Series to the Arizona Diamondbacks in seven games.

MVP

By the end of the season, Ichiro had broken at least 13 major-league, American League, or Mariners records. He was named the Rookie of the Year and the Most Valuable Player for the American League, a combination no one had managed since Fred Lynn in 1975. Ichiro was pleased to have his accomplishments recognized, including the great defensive skills that won him a Gold Glove. He had committed just one error all season. Rookie of the Year was a little embarrassing—after all, he had been a pro in Japan—but he was a major-league rookie, playing in unfamiliar circumstances. Most Valuable Player, the biggest of the awards, was the greatest surprise. Most often, the award goes to a slugger, and Jason Giambi, then of the Oakland Athletics, seemed likely to win it, as he had in 2000. Mariner Bret Boone, with 141 RBIs, had also been mentioned as a possibility. Yet Ichiro really had been the most valuable player. His teammates had said he was "the driving force on this team" and "the engine of our team." Ichiro had been MVP three times in Japan, but he said, "They cannot be compared." He felt honored by the award but hastened to promise that he hoped to play even better in 2002.

Ichiro ended his baseball season with a three-day trip to the Baseball Hall of Fame in Cooperstown, New York. During the season he had said he was especially excited to see the historic stadiums of the United States. It seemed fitting to him that he end his first season in a place where he could learn more about the history of baseball in America and about the game's great players. People were already saying he might be one of them.

Rob Dibble ended his baseball season with an online article called "Eating Crow, Thanks to Ichiro," in which he said he would make good on his promise to run around Times Square naked if Ichiro won the batting title. (The Speedo he wore was cheating but perhaps necessary to avoid arrest.) He ended his article, "Ichiro, I'm sorry I ever doubted you. Welcome to America, we're glad to have you here."

6

2002–2003: High Expectations

Ichiro had a dazzling rookie year. He was the idol of two nations, a star, the hero of his team and also of Little Leaguers, who imitated his expressionless contortions as he came to the plate. At the 2001 Little League World Series, young American players, instructed to introduce themselves and name their favorite player had said, almost without exception, "My favorite player is Ichiro."

Throughout the 2001 season, Ichiro had been the subject of predictions. After all, if he was hitting so well in his first year, what might be possible in the future? Former Mariner Alex Rodriguez, then playing for the Texas Rangers, said at the 2001 All-Star break, "I wouldn't be surprised if he hit .400 in the near future, and if he played on turf, it would be .450." Ichiro had performed far better in his first year than anyone expected. By his second season, people expected Superman.

THE MARINERS SLUMP

For the first half of the 2002 season, Ichiro was still "Ichi-Hero," hitting .357, but after the All-Star break he went into a long slump. The Mariners did, too. They had been in first place in the division but finished third. Ichiro hit a respectable .280 for the second half of the season, ending with a .321 batting average. He scored 111 runs and stole 31 bases. Toward the end of the season, members of the press still called him the "Hitting Machine." Manager Lou Piniella said of him, "Ichi's more confident. He went through the wars last year, and I don't think he has any doubts now. . . . He knows now he belongs." Yet his numbers were not as good as in his rookie year. He worried about getting his 200th hit of the season. Having done it once, he expected to do it again and believed the fans expected him to do it again. He ended up with 208 hits, not the 242 of 2001.

The Mariners had lost steam. They also lost Lou Piniella, who left at the end of the 2002 season to manage the Tampa Bay Devil Rays, possibly because he disagreed with the Mariners' management policies of not signing enough good free agents and not making late-season trades.

The 2003 season was even worse. After a slow start to the season, Ichiro rebounded a bit and even hit his first major-league grand slam, on July 18 at Kansas City. Again, he slumped, hitting only .243 in the second half. He still finished the season with a .312 batting average and 212 hits, but for Ichiro nothing is more important than constant improvement. He was ashamed. He told his friend Leon Lee, manager of the 2003 BlueWave team, "It was killing me that I was letting my teammates down. I felt so much anger and anxiety at times

Ichiro hit for a double here against the Oakland A's on September 20, 2003, in Oakland. During the game, he got his 200th hit of the season and afterward cried with relief. He was feeling the pressure to meet the expectations of his spectacular rookie season. In 2002 and 2003, Ichiro started out each season on fire but slumped in the second half.

that I threw up." Lee suggested that he not worry so much and that he accept that he was still developing as a player. It was advice Ichiro had trouble taking. At night he would dream he was getting a hit and then wake up full of disappointment. When he did get his 200th hit of the season, on September 20, he cried. "I've never cried before over getting a hit. That's how much it meant," he told Narumi Komatsu. No one knew. The sunglasses he wore in the outfield hid his tears. The player famous for his "cool" did not want fans, opponents, or reporters to know how he felt. He was supposed to show his "fighting spirit," not his emotions.

Sports columnists did not know what to make of Ichiro's performances at the end of the 2002 and 2003 seasons. Perhaps the Major League Baseball season was indeed too long for him. Perhaps he wore himself out training so hard. Perhaps instead of Ichiro learning what to expect from the pitchers, pitchers were learning what to expect from Ichiro. For a while, it seemed as if he would be more likely to fly out on an inside fastball.

Opposing teams, however, mostly felt the way they always had about Ichiro. As Grady Little, the Red Sox manager at the time, said in 2002, "There's no secret way to get him out. All you can do is concentrate on the other eight guys." After all, Ichiro still led the major leagues in 2003 in multi-hit games, and he had hit 13 home runs—his career high up until that point. If he had not had such an outstanding rookie year, if he did not have seasons that were so much stronger in the first half than in the second, then he would just have been another successful baseball player.

Ichiro would conclude that his worries about his responsibility to his team and about meeting the expectations he had created in his rookie year caused him to try too hard. He "sort of lost focus," he said later, observing that hitting is always a complicated combination of patience and aggression. Because he worried so much, he was not patient enough, and he started to think so much about solving the problem that he overcorrected his stance. He was thinking so hard that he got in his own way.

THE IMPORTANCE OF ROUTINE

What got Ichiro through the harder parts of 2002 and 2003 were a lifetime's worth of habits and training. He struggled, but he still had his daily rituals, his way of preparing for a game or an at-bat, his way of winding down afterward, and his attitude toward being a ballplayer. These did not save him from worry or pain, but they helped get him through.

Ichiro is famous for his unvarying pregame warm-ups. He gets to the field early and stretches for hours, without pausing, listening to music. He runs. He lifts weights. He watches videos of the pitchers he will be facing that day. He gets a massage before every game. Before each at-bat he performs the exact same series of stretches, squats, wiggles, and practice swings. It is a routine, says Robert Whiting, "designed to keep him relaxed, to empty his mind, and, at the same time, to prevent himself from looking at the opposing pitcher before he [is] ready to mentally confront him."

Once he is in the batter's box, Ichiro also has an unvarying routine. He swings the bat over his head with one arm, then points it at the pitcher. With his left hand, he tugs the right shoulder of his uniform sleeve. He pulls the bat back and takes a breath. Then he is ready.

Ichiro believes a baseball player must be prepared mentally and physically, and he must be consistent in his preparation. "You don't turn in a spectacular performance because you happen to be in supreme condition that day," he told Brad Lefton, speaking in Japanese. "It's the times when you're in a normal mental state that you have a chance to turn in a great performance. If you allow yourself to drift out of normalcy because of pressure or frustration or some other factor, that's when things can go wrong"—as they did for him at the end of 2002 and 2003. Preparation, to Ichiro, means "an appropriate diet,

Ichiro is well-known for his pregame warm-up routine, during which he stretches for hours. Before every at-bat, too, he performs the same series of stretches and moves. The routine, one writer says, keeps Ichiro relaxed.

the proper amount of sleep, daily conditioning, and so on." Mariners trainer Rick Griffin noted that Ichiro reported for training in the spring of 2004 weighing 170 to 171 pounds (77 kilograms) and still weighed 170 to 171 pounds at the end of the season, having paid attention to all he had eaten throughout the season. Most players lose weight if they have been playing regularly and gain weight if they have not, Griffin says.

Ichiro is, after all, the player who, when tested at age 17, was already able to maintain calm under pressure. Clearly from what he says about his feelings at the end of 2003 season, he *feels* emotions—he simply does not believe in showing them. Most of the time, he can control his emotions so his game is not affected. That control, though, comes from his upbringing, from hard work, and from his attitude toward the game. He does not think he will play better if a bad game or a bad at-bat makes him lose his temper and break furniture. He believes he should be focused and calm. One catcher noticed that Ichiro exhales softly when he is at bat rather than gritting his teeth.

BAT AND GLOVE

Ichiro is also known for his care of his equipment before and, especially, after games. It helps him, and he can explain why.

During a game in July 2002 against the Anaheim Angels, Ichiro botched a bunt and caused a force-out at second, then got caught in a rundown trying to steal. The Mariners lost the game, and Anaheim knocked them out of first place in the division. It was, Ichiro said later, "not just my worst game in America, but the worst game I can remember in my professional career."

After the game, Ichiro did what he does at the end of every game: He took care of his glove, just as his father taught him when he was a child. His gloves, three each year, are handmade for him and hand-delivered to him by Yoshi Tsubota, master glovemaker for the Mizuno company in Japan—soft, light gloves with a pocket that opens very wide for the "behind-the-back catch," says Mr. Tsubota. Ichiro likes to entertain his fans when he can.

After each game, Ichiro cleans his glove, rubs on a cream that protects the leather and keeps it supple, and then checks the webbing. Part of his ritual is practical: The glove is an important part of his equipment. Like a chef's knives, he says, the glove is what he depends on to do his work, to make money, so he has to take care of it. It is part of being a professional. He finds it unimaginable that his American teammates do not take care of their equipment, that they let their gloves dry out or sit on them, or that they sit on *his* glove right after he has cleaned it. Taking care of the glove is not just practical, however. He told Brad Lefton:

> The goal is to have no regrets at the end of every day. It would be nice to be perfect on a daily basis, but . . . that's impossible. So the goal is to be as close as possible. In order to achieve that, it is imperative to set aside a period of self-reflection each day. That's what the time with my glove represents for me. The glove is directly connected to the game. There's a special meaning in reflecting back on your day's work while paying homage to a piece of equipment that helped you. So while I care for my glove, I also reflect back on my mistakes and try to identify the causes.

"Cleaning the glove cleans the heart," he said at another time. "It's all part of a 24-hour process, in which everything—eating, sleeping properly, doing correct pregame workouts—is all intertwined."

Ichiro feels the same way about his bats, which are also made to order for him at the Mizuno factory. They are 33.5 inches long and 32 ounces (85 centimeters and 907 grams) each, and they have a slightly narrower barrel than normal. This increases his control. "I didn't want the ball striking the bat in some strange place," he says. They are made of a special kind of ash (he has experimented with a few kinds since coming to the United States), painted jet black, and polished twice to make them look darker. They are shipped from Japan shrink-wrapped to protect them and, when Ichiro unwraps them, he taps each one, near where his name is imprinted, and *listens* to the bat. (He's not very communicative about what he is listening for. He once told a reporter, "Sound.") Ichiro stores his bats in humidors so that they do not gain or lose moisture. He does not throw them down at the end of an at-bat. (When he did throw a bat down roughly, in 1995, he brought it back

Ichiro carries his glove and jet-black bat with him before a game against the Angels at Safeco Field in Seattle. Ichiro's bats and gloves are made to order for him. After each game, he undertakes a ritualistic cleaning of his equipment. "This is not only baseball equipment to me, but they are part of me. You know, part of my body," he says.

to his hotel room to clean it and, in some sense, to apologize.) Ichiro takes care of his own bats rather than letting the batboy do it. At the end of each at-bat, he wipes the bat clean. "This is not only baseball equipment to me, but they are part of me. You know, part of my body," he says. "Equipment has heart, human heart, inside it."

Although many baseball players have rituals to help them relax and focus (and sports psychologists say that such rituals are helpful, even if they look funny), most American players rarely make the effort that Ichiro does in the care of their equipment. Ichiro sometimes misses the gratitude that Japanese players have for their equipment and for the field itself. Also, he finds the American habit of spitting on the dugout floor disgusting.

Ichiro's routines also include his massage before games and his foot rub afterward, which he performs with a wooden stick or a bumpy wooden foot massager. The foot rub is like the one his father used to give him when he lived at home. According to reflexologists, different parts of the soles of the feet are connected to different parts of the body. The way Ichiro rubs his feet helps with his flexibility and circulation. Also, he says, "The bottom of your feet are very important. There's a saying in Japan that the bottom of your feet are like your heart."

CONTRACT NEGOTIATIONS

In April 2003, after getting off to a slow start for the season, Ichiro suggested to the Mariners' new manager, Bob Melvin, that he be sent down to the minor leagues. Ichiro was concerned that veteran players might give the manager a hard time if he was not contributing. Of course, no one was going to send Ichiro to the minors. Melvin just laughed and told him to do his best. Ichiro did do better and led the league in multi-hit games, but the season had still been his worst in the major leagues.

It was after this difficult season that Ichiro's contract was up for renewal. If Ichiro's agent, Tony Attanasio, and team management could not come to an agreement by December, then his demand and the team's offer would go to an arbitration panel in February. The panel would look at Ichiro's performance and what other players with his experience and skills were being paid and set his salary. This is common in baseball. Attanasio said, however, that if "they force it into arbitration, Ichiro will never voluntarily sign another contract with them." It was a matter of respect—and Japanese culture, which is based on

☆ ☆ ☆ ☆ ☆

ICHIRO VERSUS

Ichiro seems to savor a duel, and not just with pitchers. For two years now during the off-season, Ichiro has pitted himself against leading figures in the fields of science, law, theater, and fashion in a Japanese television series called *Ichiro Versus*. The show, which airs on Saturday nights, was in its second season in 2007.

In the program, Ichiro and the guest sit in plain chairs lit by a simple spotlight. Segments include an amusing psychological test, a free-flowing conversation, and a word-association game in which both participants say their first thought after hearing a word or phrase. For example, on one show with the actress Keiko Matsuzaka, the narrator said, "Workplace." Matsuzaka's response: "At times, the promised land." Ichiro's: "The only place where certain things exist." For Ichiro, the word-association game is the most challenging segment.

"It's tough but exhilarating because you have to use your head," Ichiro said in Brad Lefton's *Seattle Times* article about the program. "You're on the spot to crank out a meaningful thought in a split second. My brain's probably worked harder in these two years of taping than in my entire life combined."

ningen-kankei, the web of human relations. It was the role of the club, of the people who knew Ichiro and watched him play, to decide what he was worth to them. At the same time, he knew that the team had to balance a budget and have enough money to sign other good players.

General Manager Pat Gillick had left the Mariners. His replacement, Bill Bavasi, said it was hard to measure the worth of a player like Ichiro. He had been a major-league player for only three years, but he had been a pro in Japan. He did not hit home runs, but he continued to have more than 200 hits a season. Not only was he a great player (even during an off-year), but the team also made money from his popularity, selling tickets and merchandise and deals to broadcast Mariners games in Japan. And, as Bob Finnigan reported in the *Seattle Times,* the Mariners had owner Hiroshi Yamauchi "carefully observing how they handled Ichiro, who ha[d] become an icon as much as a player, a trailblazer for Japan League position players who want to come play Major League Baseball."

In the end, the Mariners signed Ichiro for another four years, with a contract worth $44 million. It also included the possibility of $1.25 million more in bonuses (for high numbers of plate appearances). Ichiro was pleased with his new contract. It showed that the club respected him and wanted to keep him. He was not afraid of not having enough money, and he did not care if he was earning more money than anyone else. He did need to know that he was valued.

In fact, although the team and Major League Baseball make millions from his fame, Ichiro often turns down endorsement deals—well more than $40 million worth in his first five years as a Mariner. He feels that his fans will take seriously something that uses his name and image. Also, he turned down hundreds of thousands of dollars to make a MasterCard commercial simply because the ad would have shown him signing autographs while in uniform and he does not usually do that. It is not money that motivates Ichiro.

A Year for the Record Books

During the off-season, Ichiro had gotten his mind off baseball for a while. He told interviewer Narumi Komatsu that he had become interested in art and had started collecting paintings—"bold paintings with lots of energy," he said. He had also started to think about making his own furniture, he said.

SPRING TRAINING

For a player who had struggled at the end of the previous two seasons, Ichiro seemed calm when he reported for spring training in 2004. In 2003, he felt fine when he arrived for spring training and worked hard, but he started the season in a slump. In January 2004, Ichiro found himself questioning the kind of intensely hard Japanese training he had always believed in, which takes the idea of "no pain, no gain" to an extreme. Ichiro wondered if such a concept was still true for him after so many years. Of course, he said, he still needed to run and get into shape, but in the past he had always found his batting was rusty after a month off. This year, he said later, "I swung a bat for the first time in a month, and it felt fine. I didn't feel rusty at all."

Ichiro also said that he hoped to play more for enjoyment than he had before and he hoped the fans would enjoy watching him enjoy himself. The end of the previous seasons had shown that his expectations of himself and his fans' "ridiculously high" expectations of him had created too much pressure.

SLOW START

The 2004 season did not start off well for Ichiro. During spring training, the Mariners' hitting coach, Paul Molitor, and Manager Bob Melvin talked to Ichiro about the importance of his on-base percentage. They wanted him to hit less aggressively, to take more pitches, and to be willing to walk more often. It is reasonable advice for a leadoff hitter, but it was not the right advice for Ichiro. He hit only .255 in April. After that, Molitor concluded that "we were probably a little misguided." He told Ichiro to do whatever made him comfortable, so Ichiro went right back to taking very few walks.

Robert Whiting, the Japanese baseball historian, believes that, in 2004, Ichiro was able to take Leon Lee's advice. After Ichiro told Lee how upset he was by his lack of hitting at the end of 2003, Lee said, "Don't worry." He also said, "What you should be doing is easing up and trying to hit more to left field. Hit inside out and you'll be fine." That is what Ichiro began to do in 2004, said Whiting, who followed Ichiro's season on television.

Cleveland pitcher Rich White described Ichiro's hitting as his "slashing, running, swinging, hit-everything-in-the-zone

In a game against Texas in April 2004, Ichiro watched his bunt roll foul. Ichiro's season got off to a slow start, and he hit only .255 in April. Soon, though, he would be piling up the hits.

style." From time to time, it would seem that pitchers could control his hitting. They never could for long. Cleveland pitcher C. C. Sabathia said, "All you can do is make your pitches and hope he hits it at somebody. I throw him pitches in, pitches out. He hits them to left, hits them to right, hits them everywhere. There's simply no way to pitch him, and no way to defend him." Or, as Japanese fan Isao Ogata said, "The way he hits is just like a samurai. I'll bet he could split a mosquito with a sword."

As a huge number of reporters, teammates, and opponents had said during Ichiro's rookie year, he seemed to adjust to whatever a pitcher did, almost to predict what a pitcher would do. That is why baseball historians, reporters, and fans began to speak—again, as they had in 2001—of Ichiro breaking an 84-year-old record: George Sisler's 1920 record of 257 hits in one season.

SISLER'S RECORD

The possibility of Ichiro breaking Sisler's record had been raised in 2001, when Ichiro's number of hits started to near the 200 mark. In 2002 and 2003, he had gotten his 200 hits, but he had had dry spells. In 2004, Ichiro got his 200th hit on August 26 with a home run against the Kansas City Royals. He had plenty of time left to challenge Sisler. Ichiro had experienced a "breakthrough" in his hitting.

During batting practice on July 1, Ichiro thought of making a small change to his stance. He found himself more comfortable hitting than he had been in years, ending up with a .432 batting average for the month. "The 50 hits I got in May and the 50 hits I got in July and August are completely different," he told Brad Lefton. In May, he was surprised how well he was hitting. He could see mistakes in his own performance, even if no one else could. Of July and August, he said, "I could clearly explain to you why I was able to hit each pitch."

Lefton wrote that it was possible to see three differences in Ichiro's stance: "His front foot is farther off the plate, his

George Sisler of the St. Louis Browns is shown at bat in September 1920, the year he set the major-league record for most hits in a season. Two years later, he batted .420. As Ichiro got more and more hits in 2004, people wondered if he would be able to break Sisler's record.

stance is narrower, and the bat is in a more reclined position as opposed to pointing skyward." Ichiro told him, "The change I made before the game on July 1st gave me a completely fresh feeling at the plate."

GEORGE SISLER

Sisler was born in 1893 and died in 1973, the year Ichiro was born. He was a first baseman for the St. Louis Browns, nicknamed "Gorgeous George." In 1922, he hit .420, the third-highest season average in baseball's modern era. He was also a fast base runner and a great defensive player. Sports historian Bill James said that, in 1920, the year he set the season record for hits, Sisler was "about as great of a player as you can be." Three years later, Sisler developed a serious sinus infection, a generation before antibiotics were discovered to treat infections. The illness affected his eyesight, giving him double vision, and Sisler missed a whole season of baseball. Although he returned to the game and played until 1932, he was a solid player rather than a brilliant one.

Sisler was practically unknown by 2004. He had played in the era of Ty Cobb and Babe Ruth, men who were louder and more colorful on the field and in their private lives than he was. Sisler was a quiet man. The home-run hitters of his era were remembered, but he was not.

SMALL BALL

This preference for swatters over nibblers was evident in 2001 when Ichiro won the American League MVP. Even he had expected it to go to Jason Giambi or teammate Bret Boone, both home-run hitters. It remained true toward the end of the 2006 season, when David Ortiz, the Boston Red Sox's designated hitter, in an ungracious moment, argued that he, as a home-run hitter, won more games and was more valuable than a consistent all-around player like Yankee team captain Derek Jeter. It was not surprising that, when the Japanese slugger Hideki Matsui left the popular Yomiuri Giants to join the New York Yankees in 2003, some of the Japanese spotlight turned to Matsui. He was the first Japanese home-run hitter to come to the United States and challenge power pitching with power hitting. Ichiro does not play power ball. Rather he plays a game that he himself would say is Japanese style, based on mental discipline and skill rather than power.

What all this means is that many people did not consider Sisler's hits record an important one, even once they had heard about it. The record was not showy or obviously exciting like the home-run duel in 1998 between Mark McGwire and Sammy Sosa. Multiple hits in a season is a record that can be obtained only by hitting consistently and patiently and by not taking a lot of walks. "It surprises me that not more national media is here," Bob Melvin, the Mariners' manager, said. "It's one of the great records of all times. Look at the top five. Four of them played back in the 1920s."

Ichiro says that players who pay too much attention to records get themselves into trouble. Still, he wanted this one. The Mariners and their fans wanted Ichiro to break the record, too, since not much else good was happening to the team. After finishing 2001 with a record-setting 116 wins and 46 losses, the Mariners would end 2004 at 63–99. The team had gone into the All-Star break 17 games out of first place in its division, and it did not do any better afterward. Ichiro's pursuit of Sisler's record was the only reason—aside from the retirement of the popular Edgar Martinez—people were coming to Safeco Field.

Sisler's family was also excited about the possibility that Ichiro would break the record. It meant that their name, once famous in baseball, was being remembered again. (Two of Sisler's sons also played major-league ball, and a third had been an administrator.) As Ichiro approached the record, the Mariners flew Sisler's daughter, 81-year-old Frances Sisler Drochelman, and some of Sisler's grandchildren to see the games.

258

On October 1, Ichiro entered the Mariners' 160th game, against the Texas Rangers, with 256 hits. He had missed several chances on the team's recent road trip to get a hit. Safeco Field was packed—45,573 people.

In the first inning, Ichiro performed his usual warm-ups in the on-deck circle. By the time he was announced, the fans were on their feet and cheering. So many fans had cameras that the whole stadium twinkled with flashbulbs. Ichiro let a strike go by, then fouled off the next two pitches from Ryan Drese. He hit the next pitch only 10 feet to the left of home plate, but it bounced over the head of the third baseman for the tying hit—No. 257. The standing ovation lasted more than two minutes as fireworks exploded and people cheered. Time had to be called for Ichiro to acknowledge the crowd, raising his batting helmet to the fans.

In the third inning, Ichiro came to bat again. The count was full when Ichiro was able to bounce a hit past the shortstop for the record-breaking 258th hit. This time, play stopped for an even longer period. As more fireworks exploded and the theme music from the baseball movie *The Natural* played, the whole Mariners team ran to first base to grin, yell, pat Ichiro's back, and rub his head. The first baseman shook his hand. Manager Bob Melvin, right out there with his team, said later, "Goosebumps aren't even the right word. The second hit almost brought tears to my eyes." It did bring tears to the eyes of Sisler's daughter, and Ichiro walked over to the seats on the first-base line where she was sitting with four other members of the family. Ichiro bowed and shook hands with each of them and thanked them for coming to Seattle. One of Sisler's grandsons, Bo Drochelman, said after the game, "My grandfather really respected the game of baseball. He cherished it and played every minute to the hilt. That's the part of Ichiro I think he would have loved, a man dedicated to the game."

Mariners manager Bob Melvin hugged Ichiro, while his teammates and the fans cheered, after Ichiro got his 258th hit of the 2004 season to break George Sisler's record. Also that year, Ichiro became the first major-league player to have more than 200 hits in each of his first four seasons, and he was the first major leaguer to have three 50-hit months in one year.

After speaking to the Sisler family, Ichiro returned to first base, raising his helmet again and again as fans chanted, "I-CHI-RO! I-CHI-RO!" His usual mask was off. He smiled, breathed a sigh of relief so great you could see it on the TV coverage, and then looked moved. "It's definitely the most emotional I have gotten in my life," Ichiro said. "It's definitely the highlight of my career."

The ball from hit No. 258, Ichiro's bat, and the first-base bag were taken away to be given to the Baseball Hall of Fame.

Ichiro would achieve hit No. 259 later in the game, having broken two records that night: the Sisler record for the most hits in one season and New York Giant Bill Terry's 1929–1932 record for the most hits in four seasons. Ichiro had 921 to Terry's 918. Ichiro now held the records for the most hits in one season in the United States and Japan.

Fans in Tokyo and elsewhere in Japan watched the game in sports bars and on outdoor television screens. His father, Nobuyuki Suzuki, interviewed in Japan, said, "You can tell how happy and proud I am just by looking at me. The tears just won't stop flowing." Even the prime minister of Japan, Junichiro Koizumi, had a message for Ichiro: "I would like to give him my heartfelt congratulations. He has made extra efforts in addition to having a natural gift."

The prime minister understood something important about Ichiro: that his performance is always based on "extra efforts" and not just on "a natural gift." The prime minister, however, misunderstood something else. He wanted to present Ichiro with the People's Honor Award, which is given to Japan's national heroes. He had already offered this award to Ichiro when he was voted MVP after his first year as a Mariner. For the second time, Ichiro turned it down. He says he would like to receive the award after he retires. To accept it now would suggest that he has nothing left to achieve. It might take away his drive.

Ryan Drese, who was pitching for the Rangers when Ichiro got the record, said it did not bother him to give up hit No. 258. "It's not like it's the 500th home run or something like that. It's just a little single on the ground." He added that there was very little any pitcher could do to prevent Ichiro from hitting.

That game was really the end of the year for Seattle, although the season would not officially end until October 3. Ichiro completed the season with 262 hits and a .372 batting average, leading the major leagues. He had hit 225 singles, breaking the record of 206 set in 1898 by Wee Willie Keeler. His

145 hits on the road broke a record, too—Harry Heilmann's 1925 record of 134.

Earlier in the 2004 season, Ichiro had broken other records. On August 25, he became the first player in the majors to have 200 or more hits in each of his first four seasons. On August 28, he became the first major-league player to have three 50-hit months in one season. That August he batted .463.

When the 2004 season was over, Manager Bob Melvin was fired. After the Mariners' disastrous first half of the season, management released some older or unproductive players and

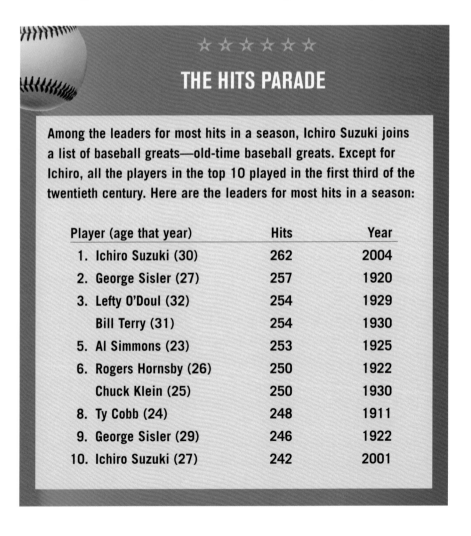

★ ★ ★ ★ ★

THE HITS PARADE

Among the leaders for most hits in a season, Ichiro Suzuki joins a list of baseball greats—old-time baseball greats. Except for Ichiro, all the players in the top 10 played in the first third of the twentieth century. Here are the leaders for most hits in a season:

Player (age that year)	Hits	Year
1. Ichiro Suzuki (30)	262	2004
2. George Sisler (27)	257	1920
3. Lefty O'Doul (32)	254	1929
Bill Terry (31)	254	1930
5. Al Simmons (23)	253	1925
6. Rogers Hornsby (26)	250	1922
Chuck Klein (25)	250	1930
8. Ty Cobb (24)	248	1911
9. George Sisler (29)	246	1922
10. Ichiro Suzuki (27)	242	2001

called up more than 12 players from the minors. Still, those sort of lineup changes do not quickly improve a team.

In October, the Mariners hired a new manager, Mike Hargrove. Hargrove had seen Ichiro and Hideki Matsui play in Japan at the end of the 1990s and had predicted that neither would succeed as everyday players in the major leagues. (Ichiro does not appear to hold this against Hargrove, nor does Hargrove still believe it.) The Mariners had a reputation for refusing to sign expensive players, but during the off-season, they signed two experienced, successful, and expensive free agents, first baseman Richie Sexson and third baseman Adrián Beltré.

A THANK-YOU PRESENT FROM MR. YAMAUCHI

Later in the off-season, Mariners (and Nintendo) owner Hiroshi Yamauchi gave Ichiro 5,000 shares of Nintendo, worth $109 each. It was a gift for breaking Sisler's record. Ichiro joked that he would have to get a subscription to the *Japanese Financial News* to keep an eye on his investment.

Although Yamauchi has never seen the Mariners play (he does not watch baseball), he says he will come to see them if they ever go to the World Series. He does follow the team, especially its Japanese players. Each year the team's Japanese players go to Tokyo to meet with Mr. Yamauchi, to thank him for employing them, and to promise to work hard.

Ichiro appreciated Mr. Yamauchi's gift and thanks. Still, 2004 had been a bad year for the Mariners. The record excited Ichiro, but he wanted his team, not just himself, to play well.

2005–2006: The More Things Change . . .

By 2005, there was little left of the team that had signed Ichiro in 2001. The preseason coverage acknowledged that Ichiro was pretty much responsible for helping ticket sales, not to mention sales of Mariner merchandise with his name, picture, or number on it. He also was a big part of the reason for Major League Baseball's six-year, $275 million deal to broadcast games to Japan. About 81,000 Japanese tourists still came to Seattle each year to see him play.

THE PRIVATE ICHIRO

From his early days in the United States, Ichiro had been famous for his reluctance to talk to the media. He continues only to talk to the press, if at all, in 15-minute periods, sitting at his locker, often with his back to reporters. Although he

Ichiro and Yumiko Suzuki attended a Seattle SuperSonics basketball game in November 2004 at Key Arena in Seattle. The couple is seen out in public, but in his discussions with the media, Ichiro has kept most of his off-the-field life private.

speaks to his teammates in English (and some Spanish), he talks to the media through a translator. Even when he speaks to some interviewers he has known for years, he still speaks carefully, trying not to say anything that will be misunderstood. He also is concerned that he says only what he has a right to say. Reporters who ask him how something he has done will make others view him should know by now that Ichiro never answers those kinds of questions. He will not speak for others. He will speak to interviewers he trusts about matters concerning his baseball playing and even, sometimes, his feelings about his baseball playing. But most of his life is kept private. He has a wife and a brown and white Shiba dog named Ikkyu. He travels with his wooden foot massager and a special pillow (stuffed with buckwheat) and he cannot sleep properly if the room is not completely dark. But that is nearly all that he wants the public to know about him. He could get more endorsements and he could be better known. He does not want either.

People who do know Ichiro well, including agent Tony Attanasio, former manager Bob Melvin, and Starbucks chairman Howard Schultz, who is an old friend, respect Ichiro's wishes for privacy. They say that he is a lovely, warm man who gives a great deal to charity. Then they clam up.

And so Ichiro remains, as he has always been, somewhat mysterious. He is, as one reporter said early in the 2005 season, "a player so cool that he wears onto the field a pair of space-age silver-trimmed sunglasses that are designed to hold downloaded songs and play them through tiny earpieces, but he shuns attention."

ICHIRO THE BALLPLAYER—2005

As a player, Ichiro remained largely unchanged. He tinkered with his batting stance. He did his warm-ups and practice rituals carefully. He avoided walks. "I don't know of many fans who go to the ballpark to see a hitter draw a walk," he told Brad

Lefton. In 2005, he would again hit over .300 (barely) and get 206 hits. His season was marred by a slump in late July and early August in which he went hitless in 19 at-bats. For the first time, he was not a starter in the All-Star Game, although he played in it.

Still, Ichiro continued to break the type of records that could be broken by getting many hits and few walks and seldom missing a game. On June 14, he became the third major-league player to get his 1,000th hit in fewer than 700 games. On July 30, he became the player to get the most hits (1,058) in his first five seasons of major-league play. Rather than his records inspiring the team—for the fourth year in a row it seemed that nothing could inspire the Mariners—Ichiro had to set personal goals so that he had something to work toward. Trying to live up to his belief that the fans should be entertained even if a game does not count, he hit 15 home runs and 12 triples, both career highs for him. He preferred to be working toward post-season play, but the Mariners again came in last in their division, again losing more than 90 games.

"Ichi didn't seem very happy this year," said a teammate at the end of the season. "He wasn't himself. . . . He was kind of isolated." Attanasio said that he did not know if Ichiro was sad. Maybe "tired," Attanasio said. Ichiro was not satisfied with how he played or how the team played. He had been through two general managers and three field managers in five years, and journalists wondered if current manager Mike Hargrove understood or accepted Ichiro's style of play. Besides avoiding walks, he avoids collisions and diving for the ball as much as possible, because an injured player cannot contribute to the team.

ICHIRO SPEAKS OUT

At the end of the 2005 season, Ichiro did something uncharacteristic: In an interview with the Kyodo News Service, he criticized the Mariners. The criticisms were about as polite as criticisms could be. He did not single out any player or coach by name. But as a senior member of the team, he had, by Japanese custom, both the right and the responsibility to speak up. Mostly he said that he felt that the team—coaches and players—should not give up halfway through the season when they were not doing well. He said he missed postseason play and disliked having only his own statistics to work on rather than team goals. Reporter Keizo Konishi added to the criticism by saying that he himself thought the Mariners should not be playing cards in the clubhouse right up to game time. Instead they should be studying videos of the pitchers they would face that day. (That observation appeared in Seattle papers as something Ichiro had said.) Ichiro said to a Seattle paper that some of the problems were ones that fans could not see, like whether players had "a positive feeling at the plate." When there's a 3-1 count on them, they should still be hoping to crush the next pitch, not hoping for a walk.

The response to Ichiro's comments was mixed. Center fielder Jeremy Reed said that "being serious and sitting at a locker" worked for some people and not for others. Pitcher Bobby Madritsch agreed with Ichiro that the team lacked morale. Columnist Art Thiel wrote an article, entitled "Ichiro's Words Were Long Overdue," that said that, even after several years of bad losses, little responsibility or leadership seemed to be coming from owners, managers, coaches, or players.

THE WORLD BASEBALL CLASSIC

In 2006, before Ichiro got down to the serious business of baseball, he made a guest appearance on a Japanese TV show, in which he played himself—as a murderer. The show is rather like the 1970s American series *Columbo*. In it, the viewers and the bumbling detective know who committed the crime, but the detective must prove it. The show often has famous guest stars.

The baseball news early in 2006 was the inaugural World Baseball Classic, a competition among all-star teams from many countries. After the 2005 season, major-league players had to decide if they would play in the tournament. Ichiro would not say. At first it seemed like Ichiro's usual refusal to talk to the press. But as soon as he received a formal invitation from Japan's team manager, the famous home-run hitter Sadaharu Oh, Ichiro said yes. Tony Attanasio explained that, according to Japanese etiquette, Ichiro could not say he would play on the team until he had been invited. It would have been rude to assume he would be asked.

Other players said no to Oh, including Yankee Hideki Matsui. The question of playing on the teams was a difficult one for the major leaguers. Playing in the World Baseball Classic meant that they would miss all of spring training and expose themselves to injuries in games that did not count toward their season. The games, though, counted for Ichiro. He said, "I don't even care if I get hurt," a most uncharacteristic statement from a ballplayer who won't dive to catch a ball if he can help it. The Mariners did not want him to get hurt, of course, but they were willing to let their star miss spring training. "He'll be doing the exact same thing he does every off-season, working his tail off to be ready to play," Attanasio said.

For Ichiro, the World Baseball Classic offered a chance to play on a team that could win and a chance to demonstrate the strengths of Japanese-style baseball. "Baseball is a sport where the most physically imposing team doesn't always win. If Japan wins this tournament, I think it will underscore that point and validate our brand of baseball," he told Brad Lefton.

Ichiro, the player who never talked, suddenly had a lot to say, from his comments on his decision to wear old-style short pants and tall socks ("It's a pretty sharp look, if I do say so myself," he told Brad Lefton) to his dismay that the tournament would impose a pitch limit ("If this is really going to be a tournament to determine the world's best baseball team, then they should let us compete with normal rules"). For many U.S. major leaguers, the World Baseball Classic was just an exhibition series. After all, they belong to the league that thinks it can play a "world series" without challenging any other country. Other countries took the games more seriously, as did Ichiro. "Pride for your country [is] at stake," he said.

Ichiro spent the entire championship surprising people. Ten days before the series began, the man who seemed to be careful of every word he ever said got into trouble for shooting his mouth off. He said something like, "I don't just want to win. I want the people watching to feel that [our play] is beautiful and extraordinary. I want to win in a way that will make [the opposition] think that they won't be able to beat us for another 30 years." The statement may have been meant in good nature (he was laughing when he said it), but the Korean fans responded by booing him loudly and their team beat the Japanese, 3-2, the first time they met. In the second round, when Korea again beat Japan, which could have eliminated Japan from the tournament, Ichiro *screamed*. "I felt more humiliated than at any time in my baseball life," he said. The Japanese team was able to continue in the series only when Mexico beat the United States. That loss allowed Japan to advance to the semifinals, where Japan beat Korea, 6-0. Japan then faced Cuba in the final.

Ichiro has sometimes seemed aloof and emotionally chilly to American fans. He does not show his feelings. Yet he has said that he admires American players and fans for the emotion and the joy they bring to baseball. The day before the final against Cuba, he said he hoped to bring some of those emotions to his Japanese teammates.

On a Japanese team, as a senior major-league player, Ichiro emerged as a leader. He not only made key plays (he scored seven runs in eight games and hit .364), but he slid into home in a play that could have injured his shoulder. He yelled encouragement until he was hoarse and told the *Taipei Times*,

Teammates doused Ichiro with champagne after Japan defeated Cuba, 10-6, to win the inaugural World Baseball Classic in March 2006. During the tournament, Ichiro became a vocal and emotional leader of the Japanese squad.

"I think I should have been shouting more in the past. I think this kind of husky tone is pretty cool."

Japan beat Cuba, 10-6. In the noisy celebrations that followed, the team tossed manager Sadaharu Oh in the air three times, a Japanese custom, and soaked Ichiro in champagne until he yelled, "You have to respect the old guy!"—meaning himself.

The Ichiro who emerged during the games was unrecognizable, his face looked so different contorted with despair or excitement. "I have the Japanese flag on my shoulder, so that might be the primary reason that I became so emotional in these games at the WBC," he said. "Winning the WBC championship in its first year is the highest moment of my career." The man who had been described as a "stoic samurai" who "displayed all the emotion of a doorknob" came alive during the games, as a player and as a team leader. "Ichiro is not a robot, not anymore at least," wrote Jeff Passon.

And yet, he has never really been a robot, only an extraordinarily disciplined (and private) player who thinks a lot and worries. During the World Baseball Classic, he asked Oh about hitting. "Did it ever get any easier for you at the plate?" he asked. Oh said it did not, which reassured Ichiro. "I never thought that hitting would become easy," he said. If it had remained hard for Japan's greatest home-run hitter, then it was all right that it remained hard for him.

THE 2006 SEASON BEGINS

Ichiro reported to the Mariners three days after the World Baseball Classic finals. Manager Mike Hargrove said he hoped that Ichiro could continue to be a team leader now that he was back in Seattle. Oh had understood why this was unlikely. Ichiro had played Japanese pro ball and he was Japanese, so he knew how to lead a Japanese team. Still, Ichiro brought back to the Mariners his short pants and tall socks and a great deal of energy. After a slow start (.287 in April), he hit .461 from May 19 to June 13.

Although Ichiro did not come back from his Team Japan experience as a leader, his hitting did inspire some of his teammates, like left fielder Raúl Ibáñez, who said, "Ichi makes you realize what's possible"—both in hitting and defense, he added. Ichiro continued to talk as he always had about working as hard as possible. "I am like all players: I do get excited by performances that help the team. Inside you get excited when things go well, disappointed when they don't. But I always try not to show emotion." The World Baseball Classic experience had freed Ichiro to show feelings—even the Japanese press had written, "Ichiro Suzuki breaks out of his shell"—but he could not do it as a Mariner.

JAPANESE CATCHER

There was one area in which Ichiro could lead. The Mariners had a new player, Kenji Johjima, the first Japanese catcher to play in the major leagues. Johjima would face different challenges than other players because a catcher must be able to communicate with the other members of his team.

Johjima had wanted to sign with the Mariners in part to have Ichiro as his *sempai*. A sempai is the senior person in a Japanese professional relationship. The junior person is the *kōhai*. The sempai is not just a mentor. Many rules govern the behavior of each person in the relationship. (For instance, Johjima could not ask Ichiro out to dinner but had to wait until Ichiro asked him.) When Ichiro went to high school to play baseball, the underclassmen had to cook and do the laundry for the seniors. Hierarchy is important in Japanese culture, and it remains important to Ichiro. When he criticized the Mariners' poor performance, he specified that he could do so only because he was a senior player.

The problem was that Ichiro and Johjima had played against each other in Japan, and Ichiro had not liked Johjima at all. Johjima had seemed to be "brash and cocky," lacking in manners, and careless about his ballplaying. Luckily, Ichiro

Kenji Johjima celebrated with Ichiro after Johjima drove Ichiro home with a two-run homer against the Kansas City Royals in September 2006. Johjima was the first Japanese catcher to play in the major leagues. Ichiro has served as a *sempai*—the senior person in a Japanese professional relationship—to Johjima.

soon decided that he had been mistaken about his new team-mate. He found him to be "very detailed-oriented and consci-entious"—words of high praise from Ichiro. Ichiro also found Johjima to be properly respectful of him as his sempai, and the two began to train together and be friends away from the ballpark. Instead of Ichiro sitting alone in the dugout, which was always his choice, he allowed Johjima to sit next to him. Ichiro's comfort with his new teammate, like his comfort as leader of Team Japan and his relationship with team manager Sadaharu Oh, was a reminder that America and American cul-ture remained foreign to Ichiro.

2006 WINDS DOWN

The Mariners went into the All-Star break only 2½ games out of first place in their division. Still, Ichiro thought that the team was on the wrong track. "We need to look past [the number out of first] and care more about being a winning team," he said. He was hitting .343 and had six home runs, 31 RBIs, and 27 stolen bases. As usual, he was training hard before each game, long before the other players started to pre-pare. "By the time the team is stretching, I'm ready to play," he said.

After the All-Star break, the Mariners started to fall in the standings. They had long losing streaks. Ichiro would do what he could for the team, including playing center field from the middle of August to the end of the season so that Chris Snelling could play right field and add his bat to the lineup.

Ichiro also got his 200th hit, on September 16. "People take it for granted that he is going to get 200 hits," Hargrove said. "I don't know if people realize how difficult it is. If it was that easy, everybody would do it." Ichiro said that he did feel the pressure to get those hits every year, but "in the end, it gives me great joy." He broke a number of club records, including the mark for endurance (playing in 300 straight games).

Ichiro's accomplishments for the 2006 season included getting his 2,500th career hit in professional ball (including his hits in Japan) by age 32, which he did on June 13. Only Ty Cobb had ever achieved that. "I am very honored," he said. "At the same time I am happy, however, I don't want to lose anything of myself. I want to be sure I will always be myself." As always, he worries that records or awards will distract him.

The Mariners had finally brought in expensive players, but they were not playing much better as a team. Although Adrián Beltré and Richie Sexson posted respectable numbers at the end of the year, they did not get hits when needed. Their best hitting came after the Mariners were out of the pennant race. The team's pitching was also unreliable.

Just before the end of the season, the Mariners sent out a letter to season-ticket holders, telling them that the team was coming along fine, that the team had not lost as many games as it had in the last three years, and that no changes in the team management would be made. The letter was a reply to rumors that Hargrove would be replaced, and it was also in response to the concerns of season-ticket holders, who were tired of a last-place team.

Ichiro was also tired of playing on a losing team and, as he said at the All-Star break, a team that did not seem to care enough about winning. At that time, he also said of the Mariners, through his translator:

If there is a problem, we need to notice it, what creates the problem. The problem usually isn't just on the cover. You need to look much deeper. For example, if we're talking about a tree, and the tree has a problem, you need to look at the root. But you cannot see the root. The mistake is to keep watering the fruit. That is not going to solve anything. You need to find out where the problem is first.

★ ☆ ★ ☆ ★ ☆
WHY ICHIRO WON'T HIT .400

Ichiro has always had a high batting average and a high number of hits. Beginning with his first season with the Mariners, people thought that he might become the first player since Ted Williams (in 1941) to have a season batting average over .400. Major-league players, though, do not hit .400 anymore, and conventional wisdom suggests that Ichiro will not either. Why not?

1. Ichiro does not take walks and, as a leadoff singles hitter, pitchers do not intentionally walk him. Because walks do not count as an at-bat, Ichiro's distaste for the walk means that he has an enormous number of official at-bats. Over his six seasons with the Mariners, Ichiro has averaged 683 at-bats per season. To hit .400, he would need to get 273 hits—11 more than his 2004 record-breaking season.

2. Players are streaky. Ichiro has had months when he was hitting over .400. (He has had periods when he was hitting over .500.) He has also had a couple of months when he hit below .250. So the long baseball season often evens out averages.

3. In the days when players hit over .400 for the season, pitchers generally pitched entire games. No specialty pitchers came in for middle relief or to close or to get one batter out. By the seventh, eighth, and ninth innings, batters were facing a tired, familiar pitcher.

Ichiro is likely to continue to break records for at-bats, plate appearances, and numbers of hits. Some pundits believe he may be more likely to break another record thought to be unreachable—Joe DiMaggio's 56-game hitting streak from 1941—than he is to bat .400 for a season.

In a game on April 3, 2007, Ichiro headed toward third on his seventh-inning RBI triple against the Oakland Athletics. The Mariners won the game, 8-4. Ichiro's contract with the Mariners is up after the 2007 season. He has not publicly said what his plans are.

2007 AND BEYOND

Ichiro's contract with the Mariners expires at the end of the 2007 season. He will not talk to the media about what he plans to do. In the same way that he could not say he would play on Team Japan until after he was asked, he cannot say if he will stay on the Mariners. He would not discuss that with the public until he, his agent, and the owners and management have talked about it. He did end rumors that he might want to be traded before his contract was up by agreeing to continue to play center field, if necessary.

Ichiro got bored in his last year or two in Japan, playing on a losing team that no one came to watch. Of course, in Seattle, fans do come to watch him. Still, for Ichiro, winning has never been the only issue. Just before the end of the 2006 season, he told the *Seattle Times*, "I think it's true for any player that they don't want to be on a losing team. But even a winning team can't just win and not gain anything in the process. So the question is, whether you're a team that's winning or losing, are you gaining? Are you growing?" Ichiro's goal has always been to have his baseball playing improve. He wants the team to have the same attitude.

At the end of 2007, Ichiro will be 34 years old. He is in great physical shape, but he cannot play forever. The Mariners will want to sign him to the team again. Will Ichiro feel an obligation to the owner for giving him his chance in the major leagues or has that obligation been fulfilled by his years of play for the team? Will Seattle be able to offer him enough money, now that they have more expensive players on the team and may want to acquire more in the off-season?

"MAN OF GREAT EFFORT"

Ichiro's teammates called him "Wizard" during his rookie year in the major leagues because he seemed to have a nearly magical ability to hit the ball wherever and whenever he wanted. They also noted his cannon of an arm and the eerie way he seemed to start to run before he had finished hitting. As the first Japanese position player to come to the United States and as the holder of many records, Ichiro will certainly be remembered in baseball history. He is a real star and a great baseball player.

Yet Ichiro would agree that his records and his performance have been the result of tremendous hard work as well as natural ability. Yes, he was born with certain strengths, including great hand-eye coordination, but he has been working on his skills since he was three years old. Of course, most people could not play baseball as well as Ichiro does no matter how much they practiced, but as one Japanese fan says, Ichiro seems to be a "man of great effort" rather than a "man of genius." Ichiro's achievements have been the result of talent, hard work, and the ability to hold on to his own goals and values throughout his life. The achievements are ones to be proud of. His outstanding performance as the first major-league position player from Japan opened the door for other players. If he never picked up a bat again, his place in baseball history would still be secure.

STATISTICS

ICHIRO SUZUKI
Primary position: Right field (Also, CF)

Full name: Ichiro Suzuki •
Born: October 22, 1973, Toyoyama,
Japan • Height: 5'9" • Weight: 170 lbs. •
Team: Seattle Mariners (2001–present)

☆ ☆ ☆ ☆ ☆ ☆

YEAR	TEAM	G	AB	H	HR	RBI	BA
2001	SEA	157	692	242	8	69	.350
2002	SEA	157	647	208	8	51	.321
2003	SEA	159	679	212	13	62	.312
2004	SEA	161	704	262	8	60	.372
2005	SEA	162	679	206	15	68	.303
2006	SEA	161	695	224	9	49	.322
TOTAL		957	4,096	1,354	61	359	.331
Career in Japan							
1992	OBW	40	95	24	0	5	.253
1993	OBW	43	64	12	1	3	.188
1994	OBW	130	546	210	13	54	.385
1995	OBW	130	524	179	25	80	.342
1996	OBW	130	542	193	16	84	.356
1997	OBW	135	536	185	17	91	.345
1998	OBW	135	506	181	13	71	.358
1999	OBW	103	411	141	21	68	.343
2000	OBW	105	395	153	12	73	.387
TOTAL		951	3,619	1,278	118	529	.353

Key: OBW = Orix BlueWave; SEA= Seattle Mariners; G = Games; AB = At-bats;
H = Hits; HR = Home runs; RBI = Runs batted in; BA = Batting average

CHRONOLOGY

1973   October 22   Born in Toyoyama, Japan.

1976   Receives his first baseball glove.

1980   Joins his first organized baseball team.

1991   Graduates from Aiko-Dai Meiden High School; drafted by Orix BlueWave.

1991-1993   Spends most of two seasons in BlueWave minors.

1994   Named to the BlueWave starting lineup; becomes known just as "Ichiro"; establishes Japanese pro record of 210 hits in a season; wins MVP, first of seven batting titles, MSP (Matsutaro Shoriki Prize), "Best Nine" (like major-league All-Stars), and Gold Glove.

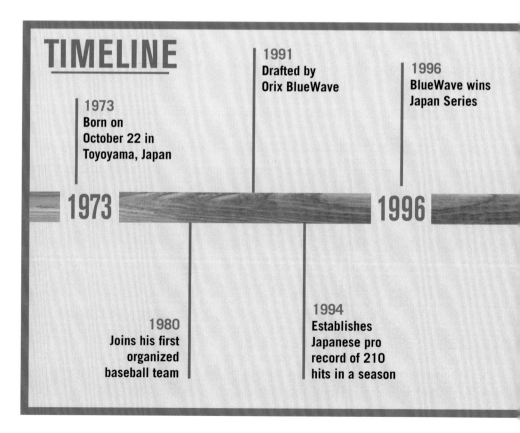

TIMELINE

1973
Born on
October 22 in
Toyoyama, Japan

1991
Drafted by
Orix BlueWave

1996
BlueWave wins
Japan Series

1973   **1996**

1980
Joins his first
organized
baseball team

1994
Establishes
Japanese pro
record of 210
hits in a season

1995   **January 17** Earthquake strikes Kobe, home of the
BlueWave; Ichiro wins MVP, batting title, MSP, Best
Nine, Gold Glove.

1996   BlueWave wins Japan Series (Japanese equivalent
of World Series); Ichiro wins MVP, batting title, Best
Nine, Gold Glove.

1997   Establishes Nippon Professional Baseball record of
216 consecutive at-bats without striking out; achieves
his Japanese career high of 91 RBIs; wins batting title,
Gold Glove, Best Nine; meets Yumiko Fukushima.

1998   Wins batting title, Best Nine, and Gold Glove for fifth
year in a row.

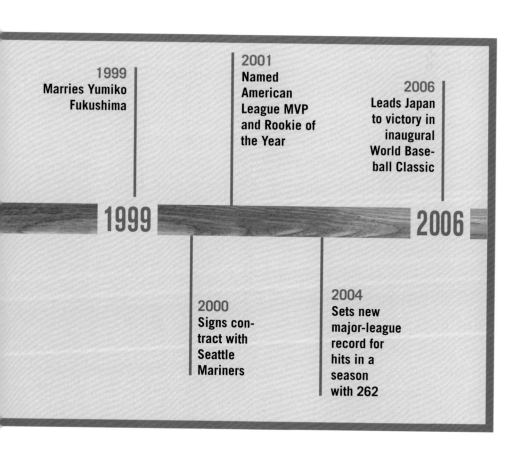

1999
Marries Yumiko
Fukushima

2001
Named
American
League MVP
and Rookie of
the Year

2006
Leads Japan
to victory in
inaugural
World Base-
ball Classic

1999   **2006**

2000
Signs con-
tract with
Seattle
Mariners

2004
Sets new
major-league
record for
hits in a
season
with 262

1999   Attends spring-training camp of Seattle Mariners; wins batting title, Best Nine and Gold Glove; marries Yumiko Fukushima in Los Angeles, California.

2000   Wins batting title, Best Nine, and Gold Glove.

November BlueWave notifies commissioner of Japanese baseball that Ichiro will be "posted" to the U.S. major leagues; Ichiro signs contract with Seattle Mariners.

2001   **April 2** Makes major-league debut; has a 23-game hitting streak from April 22 to May 18; receives record number of votes for the All-Star team; wins batting title and Gold Glove; becomes first major-league player since Jackie Robinson (1949) to lead majors in hits and steals; is named American League MVP and Rookie of the Year.

2002   Makes starting lineup for the All-Star team; gets 200 hits in a season for second year.

2003   Makes starting lineup for All-Star team; gets 200 hits in a season for third year; signs a four-year, $44 million contract with Seattle Mariners.

2004   Sets new major-league record for hits in a season with 262, breaking George Sisler's 1920 record; gets 50 hits in a month three times during the season; wins batting title, with a .372 average.

2005   **June 14** Reaches 1,000 hits in fewer games than anyone in major-league history.

July 30 Reaches 1,058 hits—the most of any player within his first five seasons of major-league play.

2006   Misses Mariners spring training to play for Team Japan in inaugural World Baseball Classic; Team Japan wins tournament.

2006   July 13 Has 2,500th hit in professional baseball
         (including Japanese and U.S. play), becoming the first
         player since Ty Cobb to do so by age 32; becomes the
         first player to have six 200-hit seasons in his first
         six years of major-league play.

GLOSSARY

arbitration   The process by which a third party settles a salary dispute between a player and a team. In baseball, the player and the team each submit a salary figure to the arbitrator. The arbitrator then picks one or the other; there is no compromise.

at-bat (AB)   An official turn at batting that is charged to a baseball player, except when the player walks, sacrifices, is hit by a pitched ball, or is interfered with by a catcher. At-bats are used to calculate a player's batting average and slugging percentage.

bunt   To bat a pitched ball very gently so that it rolls into the infield close to home plate. A bunt is usually hit by holding the bat loosely with hands spread apart, allowing the ball to bounce off the bat.

calisthenics   Physical exercises designed to strengthen muscles.

curveball   A pitch that curves on its way to the plate, thanks to the spin a pitcher places on the ball when throwing. Also known as a "breaking ball."

designated hitter   In the American League, a player who bats each time for the pitcher. There is no designated hitter in the National League. Baseball is the only professional sport in which different rules apply in different leagues. The lack of consistency about the designated hitter is an ongoing debate.

earned-run average (ERA)   A statistic that indicates the number of earned runs a pitcher gives up (on average) in a nine-inning game.

error   The game's scorer designates an error when a defensive player makes a mistake that results in a runner reaching base or advancing a base.

farm team   A team that provides training and experience for young players, with the expectation that successful players will move to the major leagues.

fastball   A pitch that is thrown more for high velocity than for movement; it is the most common type of pitch.

full count   A count of three balls and two strikes. Another strike will result in a strikeout while another ball will result in a walk.

fungo   A fly ball hit so fielders may practice catching.

games behind   A statistic used in team standings. It is figured by adding the difference in wins between a trailing team and the leader to the difference in losses, and dividing by two. So a team that is three games behind may trail by three in the win column and three in the loss column, or four and two, or any other combination of wins and losses totaling six.

leadoff hitter   The first batter listed on a team's lineup card. The job of the leadoff hitter is to get to first base any way he can—through a walk, a single, a bunt, even getting hit by a pitch—and then move into scoring position.

on-base percentage   The number of times a player reaches base divided by the number of plate appearances.

on deck   The offensive player next in line to bat after the current batter is said to be on deck. Often the player on deck will swing a weighted bat to warm up and stay in an area called the on-deck circle.

position player   A baseball player who plays any position other than pitcher.

runs batted in (RBI)   The number of runs that score as a direct result of a batter's hit(s) are the runs batted in by that batter. The major-league record is 191 RBIs for a single year by one batter.

sacrifice   A ball hit by the batter that advances the runner to the next base while the batter receives an "out" for his attempt. Examples include a sacrifice fly and a sacrifice bunt.

screwball   A pitch that curves to the same side from which it was thrown. For a right-handed pitcher, the ball would break to his right—"in" to a right-handed hitter. Also known as a reverse curve or a fadeaway.

slider   A relatively fast pitch with a slight curve in the opposite direction of the throwing arm.

BIBLIOGRAPHY

Andriesen, David. "Ichiro Breaks 84-Year-Old Record for Hits in a Season." *Seattle Post-Intelligencer,* October 2, 2004. Available online at *http://seattlepi.nwsource.com/baseball/193496_ichiro02.html*

Associated Press. "Routine Keys Ichiro's Hitting Mastery," October 2, 2004. Available online at *http://www.msnbc.msn.com/id/6159516/*

———. "258 . . . Plus One," October 2, 2004. Available online at *http://sportsillustrated.cnn.com/2004/baseball/mlb/10/01/bc.bba.suzuki.hitsrecor.ap/index.html*

Bishop, Greg. "M's Notes: Bobblehead Fever Returns to Safeco." *Seattle Times,* April 21, 2006. Available online at *http://seattletimes.nwsource.com/html/sports/2002943688_marinotes21.html*

Bloom, Barry M. "Ichiro, Oh Share Mutual Admiration." MLB.com, March 20, 2006. Available online at *http://mlb.mlb.com/news/article.jsp?ymd=20060319&content_id=1356199&vkey=news_mlb&fext=.jsp&c_id=mlb*

Caple, Jim. "The Art of Being Ichiro." ESPN.com, July 30–31, 2005. Available online at *http://sports.espn.go.com/espn/eticket/story?page=ichiro*

———. Ichiro's Bats More Than Pieces of Wood." ESPN.com, July 1, 2002. Available online at *http://espn.go.com/mlb/columns/caple_jim/1400915.html*

———. "It's All Ichiro All the Time at the Ichiro Exhibition Room." EPSN.com, November 14, 2002. Available online at *http://espn.go.com/mlb/columns/caple_jim/1460455.html*

Carpenter, Les. "The Hit King Stays Guarded." *Washington Post,* May 24, 2005. Available online at *http://www.washingtonpost.com/wp-dyn/content/article/2005/05/23/AR2005052301637.html*

Dibble, Rob. "Eating Crow, Thanks to Ichiro." ESPN.com, Oct. 4, 2001. Available online at *http://espn.go.com/talent/danpatrick/s/2001/1004/1259399.html*

Eskew, Alan. "Mariners Fall Despite Ichiro's Heroics." The Official Site of the Seattle Mariners, September 17, 2006. Available online at *http://mlb.mlb.com/news/gameday_recap.jsp?ymd=20060916&content_id=1666618&vkey=recap&fext=.jsp&c_id=sea*

Etkin, Jack. "Ichiro Mania." *Baseball Digest*, December 2001.

Farber, Michael. "Rising Son." *Sports Illustrated*, December 4, 2000.

Feiler, Bruce S. *Learning to Bow: Inside the Heart of Japan.* New York: Ticknor & Fields, 1991.

Finnigan, Bob. "Ichiro Signs Four-Year Deal." *Seattle Times*, December 19, 2003. Available online through *http://seattletimes.nwsource.com*

———. "Ichiro's on Another Upswing." *Seattle Times*, June 13, 2006. Available online at *http://seattletimes.nwsource.com/html/mariners/2003057629_mari13.html*

———. "Losing, Changes Seem to Take Toll on Ichiro." *Seattle Times*, October 18, 2005. Available online at *http://seattletimes.nwsource.com/html/mariners/2002567480_ichiro18.html*

———. "Notebook: Ichiro Gets to Share the Wealth." *Seattle Times*, February 28, 2005. Available online at *http://seattletimes.nwsource.com/html/sports/2002191928_marinotes28.html*

———. "Seattle's Ichiro Suzuki Makes It Big in the Majors." *Baseball Digest*, November 2002.

Greene, Jay, and Ken Belson. "The Mariners Catch a Tsunami." *Business Week*, June 25, 2001. Available online at *www.businessweek.com/magazine/content/01_26/b3738105.htm*

Harding, Thomas. "Ichiro: Mariners Need to Look Within." The Official Site of the Seattle Mariners, July 10, 2006. Available online at *http://seattle.mariners.mlb.com/news/ article.jsp?ymd=20060710&content_id=1551150&vkey =news_sea&fext=.jsp&c_id=sea*

Hawthorn, Tom. "The Language of Hits." *National Post*, May 8, 2001. Available online at *http://www.tomhawthorn. com/?a=22*

Hickey, John. "Glove Affair: 'He's the Best.'" *Seattle Post-Intelligencer*, March 9, 2001. Available online at *http:// seattlepi.nwsource.com/baseball/mari099.shtml*

——. "Ichiro, M's Pushing Deadline." *Seattle Post-Intelligencer*, December, 18, 2003. Available online at *http://seattlepi. nwsource.com/baseball/153027_mari18.html*

——. "Ichiro's Impact Is Immediate." *Seattle Post-Intelligencer*, March 30, 2001. Available online at *http://seattlepi.nwsource. com/baseball/bbichiro.shtml*

Kindred, Dave. "Ichiro Is a Vision of Hitters Past." *Sporting News*, October 4, 2004.

Knisley, Michael. "Follow That Star!" *Sporting News*, March 19, 2001.

Konishi, Keizo. "Reporter Aims to Get It Right." *Seattle Times*, December 4, 2005. Available online at *http://seattletimes. nwsource.com/html/sports/2002663243_japan04.html*

Lefton, Brad. "Cool. Calm. Collected. Ichiro Explained." *Sporting News*, March 6, 2003.

——. "Higher Plane: In Mariners Star Ichiro Suzuki's World, 'See the Ball, Hit the Ball' Applies on So Many Levels." *Sporting News*, May 20, 2005.

——. "Ichiro Prepares for WBC—And Better Season With M's." *Seattle Times*, February 21, 2006. Available online at *http://seattletimes.nwsource.com/html/mariners/2002818633_ichiro21.html*

———. "Ichiro, Johjima Develop Mutual Trust." *Seattle Times,* September 1, 2006. Available online at *http://seattletimes. nwsource.com/html/sports/2003238714_ichiro01.html*

McCauley, Janie. "What Major Leaguers Take on the Road, From Special Pillows to Ichiro's Massager." *Seattle Times,* July 31, 2006. Available online at *http://seattletimes.nwsource. com/html/traveloutdoors/2003165427_webathletespack31. html?syndication=rss*

Morosi, Jon Paul. "Ichiro Unhappy With M's." *Seattle Post-Intelligencer,* November 16, 2005. Available online at *http:// seattlepi.nwsource.com/baseball/248510_ichiro16.html*

Ostler, Scott. "Ichiro Continuing to Play the Game His Way." *San Francisco Chronicle,* May 18, 2006. Available online at *http://www.sfgate.com/cgi-bin/article.cgi?f=/c/a/2006/05/18/ SPGASITSRK1.DTL*

Passan, Jeff. "Ichiro's Rebirth." Sports.yahoo.com, March 20, 2006. Available online at *http://sports.yahoo.com/mlb/ news?slug=jp-ichiro032006&prov=yhoo&type=lgns*

Price, S. L. "The Ichiro Paradox." *TimeAsia,* July 8, 2002. Available online at *http://www.time.com/time/magazine/ article/0,9171,300682,00.html*

Rains, Rob. *Baseball Samurais: Ichiro Suzuki and the Asian Invasion.* New York: St. Martin's Press, 2001.

Rovell, Darren. "Tailoring Teams That Sell to a Diverse Fan Base." ESPN.com, May 13, 2002. Available online at *http:// espn.go.com/gen/s/2002/0508/1380155.html*

Saraceno, Jon. "Ichiro-Mania Knows No Bounds." *USA Today,* July 11, 2001. Available online at *http://www.usatoday.com/ sports/comment/saraceno/2001-07-11-saraceno.htm*

Schlegal, John. "Ichiro Draws High Praise From Peers."
The Official Site of the Seattle Mariners, October 2, 2004.
Available online at *http://www.mlb.com/news/article.
jsp?ymd=20041002&content_id=878907&vkey=news_
sea&fext=.jsp&c_id=sea*

Schwartz, Alan. "Suzuki's Magic Number Should Be 56,
not .406." *New York Times*, May 1, 2005.

Sherwin, Bob. "HITS-TORY! Ichiro Breaks Sisler's Record."
Seattle Times, October 2, 2004. Available online at *http://
seattletimes.nwsource.com/html/sports/2002052125_
ichiroheads02.html*

Shields, David, compiler. *"Baseball Is Just Baseball"*:
The Understated Ichiro. Seattle, Wash.: TNI Books, 2001.

——. "Being Ichiro." *New York Times Magazine*,
September 16, 2001.

Stone, Larry. "The Art of Baseball: A Tradition of Supersti-
tion." *Seattle Times*, September 25, 2005. Available online
through *http://seattletimes.nwsource.com*

——. "Ichiro Goes Deep, Keeps Roots Secret." *Seattle Times*,
July 11, 2006. Available online at *http://seattletimes.nwsource.
com/html/mariners/2003118832_starnotes11.html*

——. "The Art of Ichiro: Right Hitter, Right Time." *Seattle
Times*, September 16, 2004. Available online through *http://
seattletimes.nwsource.com*

Street, Jim. "Ichiro Commits to Play in WBC." MLB.com,
December 1, 2006. Available through *http://mlb.mlb.com*

——. "Ichiro Playing Role of 'Big Brother.'" MLB.com,
March 2, 2006. Available through *http://mlb.mlb.com*

——. "Ichiro Relishes Classic Championship." MLB.com,
March 21, 2006. Available through *http://mlb.mlb.com*

Suzuki, Ichiro. *Ichiro on Ichiro: Conversations with Narumi Komatsu.* Seattle, Wash.: Sasquatch Books, 2004.

Thiel, Art. "Ichiro's Routine Far From Ordinary." *Seattle Post-Intelligencer,* September 30, 2004. Available online at *http://seattlepi.nwsource.com/thiel/193121_thiel30.html*

———. Ichiro's Words Were Long Overdue." *Seattle Post-Intelligencer,* November 16, 2005. Available online at *http://seattlepi.nwsource.com/thiel/248518_thiel16.html*

Toronto, Jeff Pearlman. "Ichiro the Hero." *TimeAsia,* June 4, 2001. Available online at *http://205.188.238.109/time/arts/article/0,8599,129011,00.html*

Whiting, Robert. "Around the Horn." *TimeAsia,* November 11, 2002. Available online at *http://www.time.com/time/magazine/article/0,9171,389022,00.html*

———. "Catching On." *Sports Illustrated,* March 13, 2006.

———. *The Meaning of Ichiro: The New Wave from Japan and the Transformation of Our National Pastime.* New York: Warner Books, 2004.

———. *You Gotta Have Wa.* New York: Vintage Departures, 1990.

Wikipedia. "Ichiro Suzuki." Available online at *http://en.wikipedia.org/wiki/Ichiro_Suzuki*

———. "Seattle Mariners." Available online at *http://en.wikipedia.org/wiki/Seattle_Mariners*

FURTHER READING

Rains, Rob. *Baseball Samurais: Ichiro Suzuki and the Asian Invasion.* New York: St. Martin's Press, 2001.

Shields, David, compiler. *"Baseball Is Just Baseball": The Understated Ichiro.* Seattle, Wash.: TNI Books, 2001.

Stewart, Mark. *Ichiro Suzuki: Best in the West* (Baseball's New Wave). Brookfield, Conn.: Millbrook Press, 2002.

Stout, Glenn. *At the Plate With . . . Ichiro* (Matt Christopher). Boston, Mass.: Little, Brown & Company, 2003.

Whiting, Robert. *The Meaning of Ichiro: The New Wave from Japan and the Transformation of Our National Pastime.* New York: Warner Books, 2004.

WEB SITES

Baseball Almanac

http://www.baseball-almanac.com

Baseball Reference

http://www.baseball-reference.com

Japanese Baseball

http://www.japanesebaseball.com/

Major League Baseball: The Official Site

http://mlb.mlb.com/index.jsp

The Official Site of the Seattle Mariners

http://seattle.mariners.mlb.com/index.jsp?c_id=sea

PICTURE CREDITS

INDEX

ABOUT THE AUTHOR

JUDITH LEVIN has worked in publishing for 20 years as an editor and as a freelance writer. She is the author of a number of biographies, including one about Hugo Chávez for Facts on File, as well as books for children and teens on history and science. Judith has been a baseball fan ever since she helped raise a catcher and saw the hard work, patience, and concentration that the game requires.